THANK YOU

Firstly, thank you for buying this book and investing in not only me but your self-development.

I want to thank my wife, Alison, for her love and support over the past few years. Without her help, I wouldn't be in such a privileged position.

Thanks to the thousands of players and parents who have trusted me to help them, or their kids, on their journey.

The games in this book have been shaped, inspired and tested by you!

And thank you to the following people who have helped get the book up and running:

- Brendan Roberts, Pavel Duffej, Matt Wigham, Sebastian Dietrich, Rob Salmon, Stephen Garvin and Constanze Buettner.

Your generosity and donations were a great help in getting this book written.

Lastly, thank you to my nan, Rose. You gave me anything I ever needed and helped shape the person I am today.

Table of Contents

1   **INTRODUCTION TO CONSTRAINT BASED COACHING**
Understand the theory

25   **SKILL BUILDERS**
Develop Great Skills with these fun warm ups

30   **MAIN GAMES**
Both Back, Serve, Return and Net Games for Players

87   **COMPETITION**
Lets get competitive

MY TENNIS COACHING

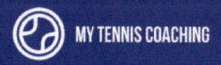

THE ART OF TENNIS COACHING

THE GAME IS THE TEACHER

THE COURT IS THE LEARNING ENVIROMENT

THE COACH IS THE FACILITATOR

WHAT IS CONSTRAINT - BASED COACHING?

In Constraint-Based Coaching (CBC), players are encouraged to discover effective movements and develop tactical awareness via playing games.

Rather than focusing on mastering technique and then attempting to use it in a game; CBC places the players in games where they must discover how to use their skills to find success in the game effectively.

The games in this book are designed to allow players the freedom to develop skills at their own rate. The games encourage players to play in all three phases, attack, defence and neutral situations.

This encourages both technical and tactical skills development. Players will better understand when to play certain shots and how.

The player leads most of the learning, and the coach is the facilitator. Using effective questioning and manipulating elements such as the task, environment or the players themselves - the coach helps guide the player to find the solution.

ADVANTAGES OF CONSTRAINT - BASED COACHING

✓ Players play the game (or modified versions) - Players develop better problem-solving skills

✓ Practice is varied, and players develop more versatile skills

✓ Implicit learning encourages better decision making

✓ CBC players perform better under stress - Less competition anxiety

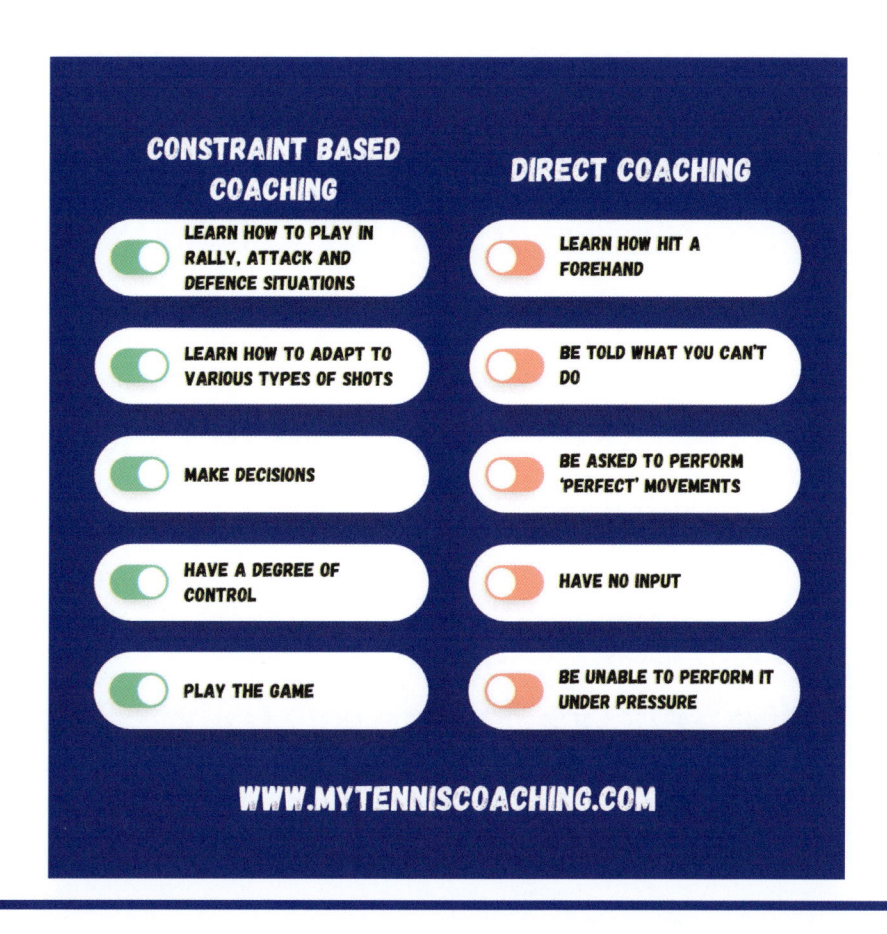

CONSTRAINT BASED COACHING	DIRECT COACHING
LEARN HOW TO PLAY IN RALLY, ATTACK AND DEFENCE SITUATIONS	LEARN HOW HIT A FOREHAND
LEARN HOW TO ADAPT TO VARIOUS TYPES OF SHOTS	BE TOLD WHAT YOU CAN'T DO
MAKE DECISIONS	BE ASKED TO PERFORM 'PERFECT' MOVEMENTS
HAVE A DEGREE OF CONTROL	HAVE NO INPUT
PLAY THE GAME	BE UNABLE TO PERFORM IT UNDER PRESSURE

WWW.MYTENNISCOACHING.COM

WHY WE NEED IMPLICIT LEARNING

Implicit Learning is where information is learnt in an unintentional manner eg learning through play.

As a young sportsman, I played multiple weekly sports, such as Football, Cricket, Basketball, Tennis and Athletics.

I also spent hours every day playing sports in school and after school, climbing trees, making camps and creating games with my friends.

Through these activities, I was developing a wide range of mental, physical and emotional skills, alongside sport-specific skills. This was implicit learning.

Physical literacy is declining in young children and they are getting less physical exercise than ever before. Children play outside less, do minor sports in school and generally specialise in one sport from an early age.

There are less opportunities for implicit learning; less demand on children to problem-solve, use physical adaptation and develop their creativity.

Traditional Tennis coaching often involves a coach leading the session; they choose the drills, give the majority of the feedback and are very technical heavy.

The opposite of the game we play.

HOW TO ENCOURAGE IMPLICIT LEARNING

So, how can coaches create an environment that develops a wide range of critical skills, such as Physical, Mental, Emotional and Tennis specific skills, in a single or small number of lessons?

The answer: Constraints Based Activity

The theory is based on the principles of non-linear pedagogy; it promotes a more hands-off approach to teaching and learning within a physical skill development setting.

Non-linear pedagogy is a teaching approach that can allow players to acquire skills more effectively.

The research on Non-linear pedagogy suggests a close connection between movement and the environment which players will find themselves in.

As Tennis is an open sport, the ball can land in multiple positions, with various ball characteristics such as height, speed and spin.

Players need to learn receiving and sending skills in more open environments and less closed or isolated situations.

CONSTRAINTS ON SKILL DEVELOPMENT

There are certain elements or factors that we are faced with as coaches and these factors will develop or hinder player development.

A coach can manipulate certain factors to enhance and improve player development.

They are

- The Player
- The Environment
- The Task

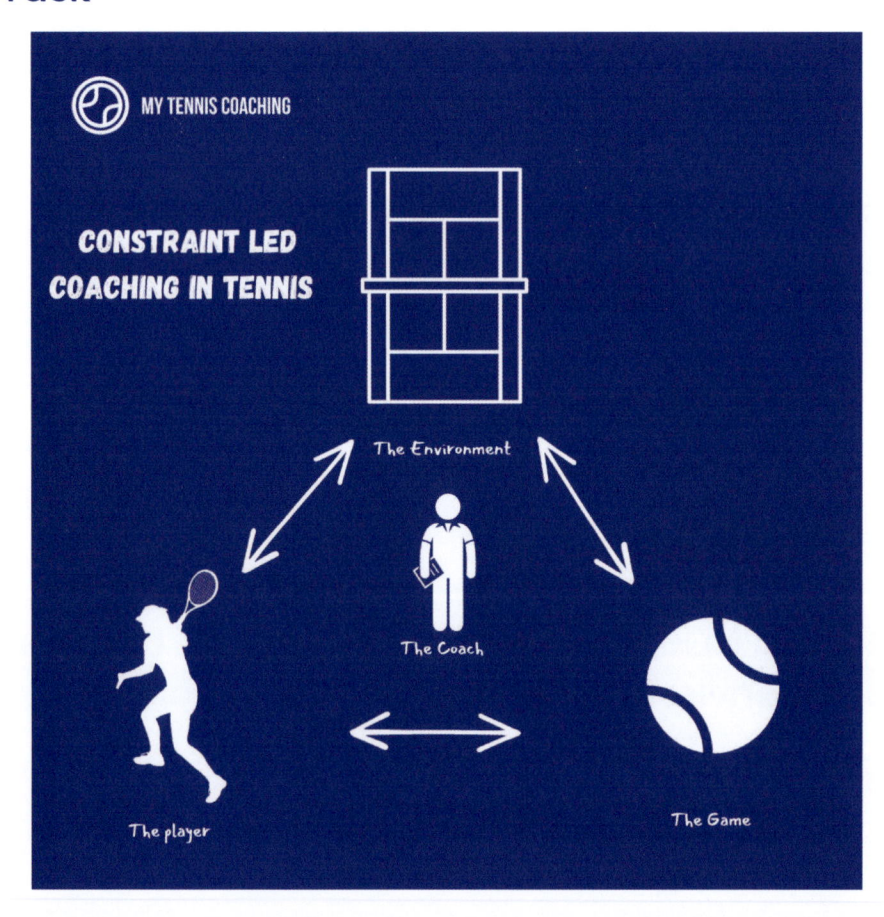

THE PLAYER

These are the players we coach; every player is an individual and has a set of personal skills.

These can be physical skills or attributes such as weight, height, fitness levels, muscle, or genetic makeup. As coaches, we may have two children aged seven but have a vast difference in physical development; one child may be taller or have more developed motor skills. Therefore, movement skills or solutions for both players should be very different.

Along with the physical aspects, psychological factors such as maturity, behaviour, motivations, and emotions must also be considered. A player's emotional level will significantly impact their learning, especially within a sporting environment.

Along with the physical and psychological skills of a player, we must consider the tennis/sporting skill levels; this may include past or current other sporting experiences. Players will have different levels of sporting experience; this needs to be factored in when designing lessons.

Many of these physical and phycological attributes we have limited control over. Still, an awareness of them can help us as coaches with our expectations within our squads and individual lessons.

PUSH V PULL COACHING METHOD

Push	Pull
Lots of Instruction	Players Facilitated
Drills & Repetitions	Skills Developed Through Games
Technique Focused	Skill Focused
Lots of Feedback	Promotes Self Discovery
Stand & Listen	Listens & Questions

FOLLOW @MYTENNISCOACHING FOR MORE TIPS

THE ENVIRONMENT

When we think of the 'environment' as a coach, we immediately think of the surroundings in which our lessons take place.

The court, the surface, and it's physical surroundings. However, we must look deeper into our learning environment, the culture we create as coaches, our values, beliefs, and how we coach and communicate.

This is often referenced as a socio-culture.

How would comparing an environment that encourages independent learning to one with more direct instruction impact skill acquisition?

The culture we create within our clubs and sessions will impact our player's learning and development.

As well as our club and coaching environments, we must also consider the impact of other external factors such as parents, peers, governing bodies etc. What are their expectations, values, and their own cultures?

How much of what we do in lessons and our coaching is impacted by these socio-cultural factors? My feeling is that it's quite a lot.

THE ENVIRONMENT

This is an area for us coaches to understand better and develop.

What learning environment do you set up, encourage, and support?

And how much do you hinder or facilitate learning in your lessons?

	EGO CLIMATE	OR	MASTERY CLIMATE
Task	OUTCOME FOCUSED GOALS		PLAYERS SET PROCESS GOALS
Authority	COACH SETS THE RULES		COACH ASK PLAYERS TO DECIDE TARGETS
Recognition	HIGHLIGHT THE BEST PLAYER		HIGHLIGHT EFFORT AND IMPROVEMENTS
Grouping	BEST PLAYERS TOGETHER		MIXED ABILITY GROUPS
Evaluation	COMPARE PLAYERS AGAINST EACH OTHER		INDIVIDUAL FEEDBACK
Time	STOP WHEN ONE PLAYER ACHIEVES THE TASK		PLAYERS CARRY ON UNTIL THEY ACHIEVE THEIR OWN TARGETS

WWW.MYTENNISCOACHING.COM

THE TASK

By far the easiest one for coaches to manipulate, we do it daily; therefore, this is arguably the most important.

The task is the games, drills, and activities we set up. We usually set the rules, equipment, court sizes, objectives, and players; therefore, it's the information we give the players during lessons.

As coaches, we can direct our players to acquire specific movement solutions by manipulating the task. For example, placing a rope of barrier tape above the net will automatically force the player to hit the ball higher. You have used the barrier tape to force players to change how they move/hit the ball.

As coaches, we can modify specific areas, including changing the space, rules, equipment and rotating players.

By modifying task constraints, we can allow the players to optimally learn movement patterns that consider their unique variations of performer constraints and how they interact with the environment and task constraints.

8U TENNIS CONSTRAINTS

At the 8 & under level, each constraint will have certain demands - things the players must be able to do. As a coach, you need to be aware of the specific demands each brings to the age group.

The demands of the environment

The environment primarily will be the practice or match court; this environment is set up and manipulated by you. However, before creating your culture or environment, it's important to find out why your players are attending, what are their goals, and what do they want from the sessions.

What are the parent's expectations and goals?

How can you as a coach combine these and create a learning environment that will satisfy all three?

We will look later at how to set up a learning environment, but the demands of the environment ultimately come down to you, the players and the parents.

THE DEMANDS OF THE GAME AT 8U

The demands of the task

At this early stage, the demands of the task are relatively quite simple to us; you hit the ball over the net. Young players however, have little or no sporting experience never mind tennis experience.

As coaches, we must focus on the basic demands of the game first. Get this right at 8 & under and you are building strong foundations for the future.

Players must be able to:

- Send and receive the ball, both underarm and overarm, after and before a bounce.
- Be aware of court boundaries.
- Be able to move, hit and recover.
- Understand serving rules.
- Understand how to win and lose a point.

THE DEMANDS OF THE GAME AT 8U

The demands of the player

The player at this stage must be able to start to work independently; be able to be set up a fun activity and be allowed to explore how to perform it.

If the player can't work without supervision, they may need to attend a parent and player squad/class.

The player will be required to use physical skills such as running, balance and throwing actions and start to develop social skills such as working with others and problem-solving.

At this age, the demands on the player are limited. Tennis should be fun and engaging, and the player should be allowed to explore and express themselves in tasks and environments suited to their age and maturity.

THE NATURAL CONSTRAINTS AT 8U

These constraints will influence how the game is played at this stage of the player pathway.

The constraints of the environment

The Ball

The 36' foam or red ball is much bigger and slower than a regular tennis ball.

It will have a consistent bounce between the knees and bottom of the rib cage when the players are trading from the baseline.

This is the ideal 'hitting zone' for these young players, therefore, making the game easier to pick up and play.

It takes much work to get the ball to bounce higher due to the constraints of the ball.

This enables players to develop their consistency and accuracy when playing.

THE NATURAL CONSTRAINTS AT 8U

The Court

The 8U court is 11m x 5.5m, the same size as a quarter of a full tennis court.

The court is relatively narrow for the player, so players need to primarily learn a little sideways and forwards.

They don't need to move backwards due to the low bounce and pace of the ball.

With this in mind, we must understand that players at this stage don't need to cover big distances, they will rarely move forwards to the net and won't find themselves pushed too far behind the baseline.

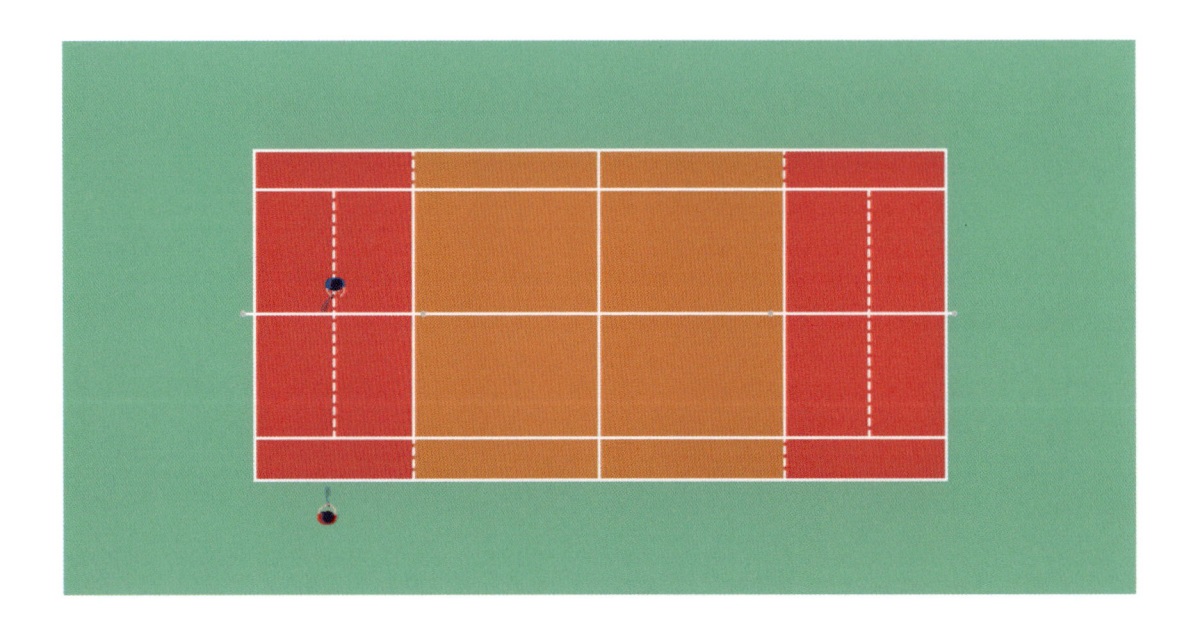

THE NATURAL CONSTRAINTS AT 8U

The Constraints of the Player

The players at this age are still developing many mental and physical skill sets. It's important that you, as the coach understand what constraints are in place on the player at that age.

Tactical Awareness

Players at this age will have a limited understanding of tactics; they may be able to find space and hit the ball away from their opponent but would need help understanding other tactical intentions such as controlling time, using their strengths etc.

An advanced player, or coming towards the end of the age group, may become more self-aware, but the majority will be very limited in this area.

The player has a limited range of understanding and will mainly be focused on the ball and themselves and not so much on their opponent.

THE NATURAL CONSTRAINTS AT 8U

Physical Skills

The player's physical literacy at this age is still in development.

Players for example will struggle to read shot balls.

This is due to the fact the eyes in an 8-year-old are different compared to a twelve-year-old; the smaller the eyes, the quicker light bounces back from the rear of the eye, making judging distance more challenging.

An 8-year-old will struggle with complex coordination and will find moving multiple body segments in a coordinated manner difficult.

This developing kinetic chain will find complex movements such as serve extremely difficult.

The young player also lacks muscle, so the use of legs to drive up into the ball is impossible.

Mental Skills

Players at this stage will find sharing challenging and are still developing social skills.

Tennis requires two players, so some cooperation must occur, i.e. players must wait for each other before starting the point.

How often do you find players start a point or activity without their partner being ready?

This is because they are still developing their awareness of working with others.

This must be taken into consideration when planning and designing activities, and a great degree of patience from the coach.

Children 8 & under will also be very kinaesthetic in their learning.

They learn by exploring and doing.

They rarely listen or watch, so your ten-minute demonstration of hitting a perfect forehand could have been a better use of time. We still must demo activities so they know what they must try, but we need to understand that they will want to have a go and explore the game themselves.

THE NATURAL CONSTRAINTS AT 8U

Tennis Skills

The lack and continued development of these physical skills will impact tennis skills.

Players at this age will need help to control time, i.e. hit the ball quicker due to a lack of physical skill and the constraint of the court and slower ball.

Players at this age will struggle with complex tennis skills and should focus on getting the ball over and in and moving their opponent.

The technical skills at this stage should be very basic, small, simple shapes.

Under 8 Tennis is the most fun, rewarding and arguably critical stage of a player's Tennis journey.

At this stage, you, the coach or parent, help develop critical skills that will last a lifetime. It's also where players fall in love with the game.

This book contains FUN tennis games where most of the learning is hidden. Let the kids play, explore and enjoy each game.

KEY TIPS

- Explain the What, Why and How.
- What the game is (Name), why we need it as a tennis player (Intention), and how (Ball characteristic).
- Allow the children to set their own targets - You just guide them. If they set a too easy or difficult target, let them adjust it after a small amount of time.
- Talk less, listen more - Let them play.
- Include the serve in every practice.
- Every game has an element of competition either individually or cooperatively.
- Encourage children to focus on the process (how) of each game and less on the outcome (result).
- Focus on what the kids <u>can</u> do when delivering feedback.
- Avoid heavy technical coaching - Let the game do the work.

TECHNIQUE ON ITS OWN IS JUST A MOVEMENT...

TECHNIQUE + PRESSURE = SKILL

MY TENNIS COACHING

SKILL BUILDERS

TIP TAP TENNIS

1. Players start close to the net.
2. Players must tap the ball over to each other.
3. Players can use forehands only, backhands only or hit alternative shots.

2 TOUCH TENNIS

1. Players must take two touches.
2. Touch one is to control.
3. Touch two is to send.
4. Players can play cooperatively or competitively.
5. Players must control the ball in front of their shoes; otherwise, they will lose control of it.

SLICE & DICE

1. Players must use a chopper grip and slice the ball.
2. One player can hit normally, and one player must use a slice.
3. Rotate players or play alternative shots.

TOUCH & SMASH

1. Players in pairs.
2. Two Touch Tennis; first touch is to control and second touch is to send.
3. First touch must go up and above the head.
4. Second touch is a smash.
5. Players must learn how to control the ball in front of their shoes.

PING PONG

1. Players in pairs.
2. Players must bounce the ball down onto their side of the court and attempt to get it over the net.
3. Great for contact point and grip development.
4. Players need a great feel to complete the task.

BODY TENNIS

1. Players in pairs.
2. Players allowed three touches of the ball.
3. At least one touch has to be with a body part.
4. The player can send the ball back with 1, 2 or 3 touches as long the body is included at least once.

HEAD TENNIS

- Players in pairs inside a half court.
- Players take turns hitting the ball.
- Players must hit the ball above head height.
- If the player hits the ball below head height or out of the box, they lose the point.

DOUBLE SWING

1. Players in pairs.
2. Players rally but must take a double swing before they hit the ball.
3. A full shadow swing.
4. A normal stroke.
5. Great for developing reading and reaction skills.

BOTH BACK

BEAT THE DICE

EQUIPMENT

- Minimum 2 players
- Ten sided dice

DIRECTIONS

1. Players have a dice between them.
2. Player A rolls the dice; whatever score they get is their rally threshold target.
3. Players attempt to rally to that number.
4. If they succeed, they score 1 point.
5. Player B then rolls the dice and gets a new target.
6. If they achieve the new target, they gain an additional point, and if they fail, they lose a point.
7. Play first to ten points wins.

IN OR OUT

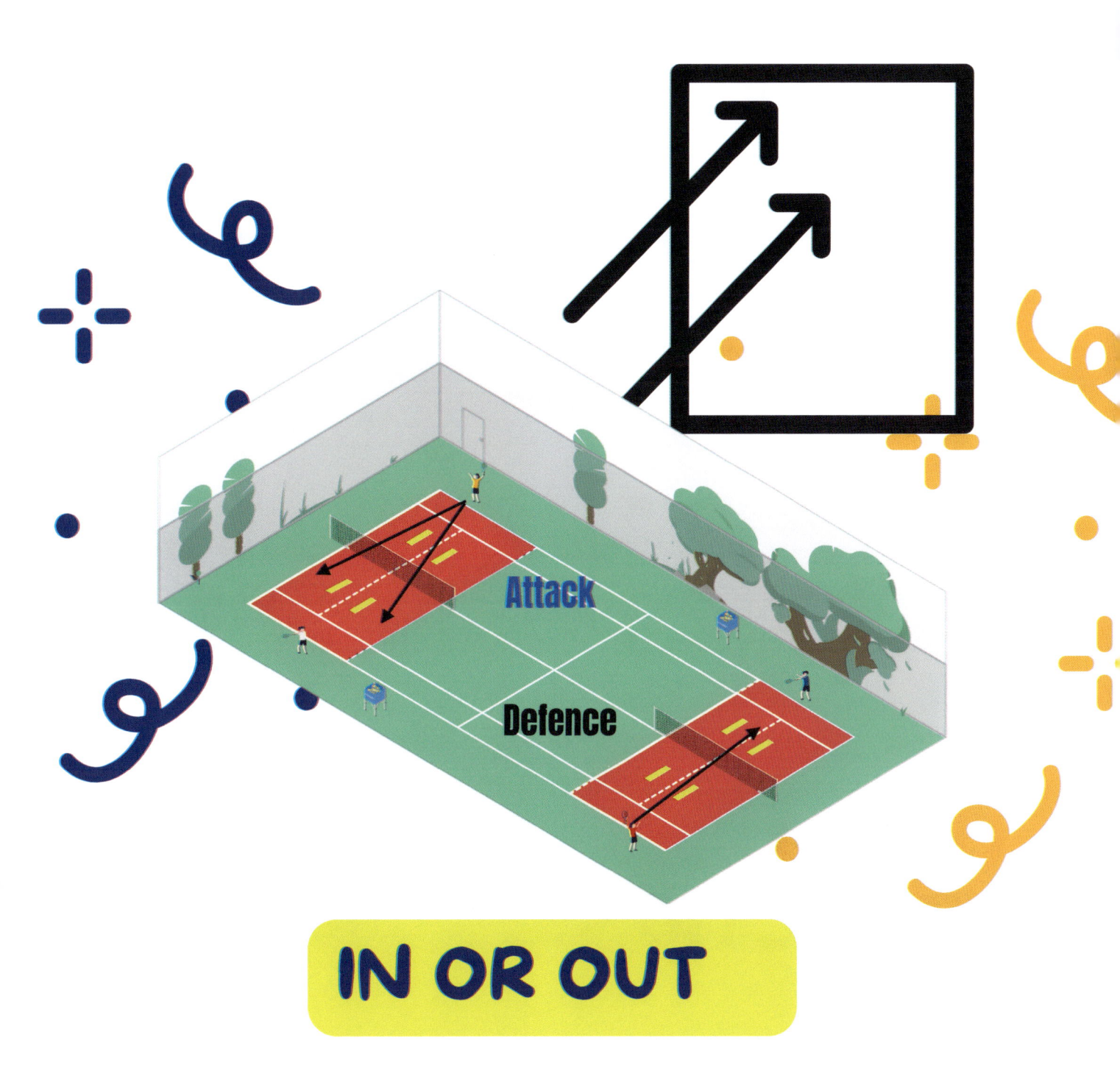

EQUIPMENT

- Minimum two players
- Throw down lines
- Cones
- Balls

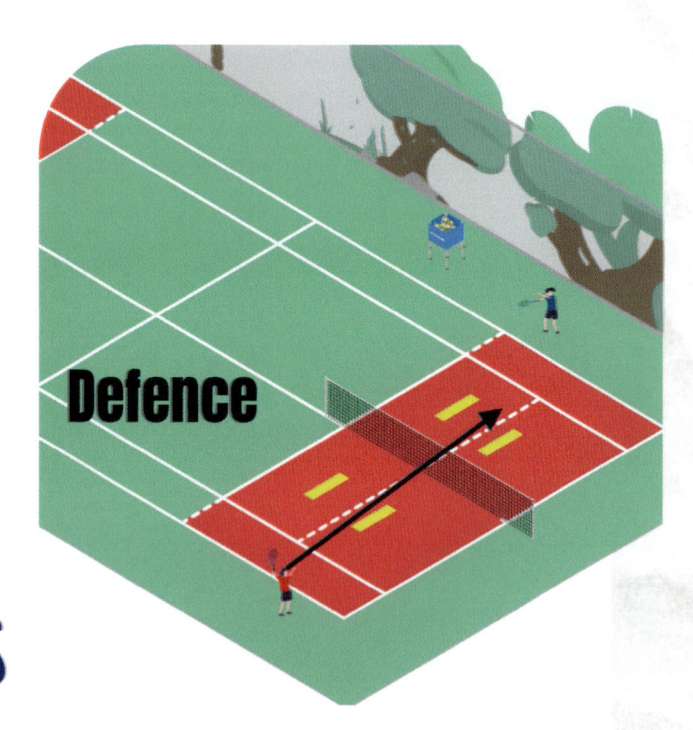

DIRECTIONS

1. Players are in pairs - One is the attacker, one is the defender.
2. The attacker must keep the ball outside the lines.
3. The defender must keep the ball inside the lines.
4. Play first to 7, then rotate positions.

DANGER ZONE

EQUIPMENT

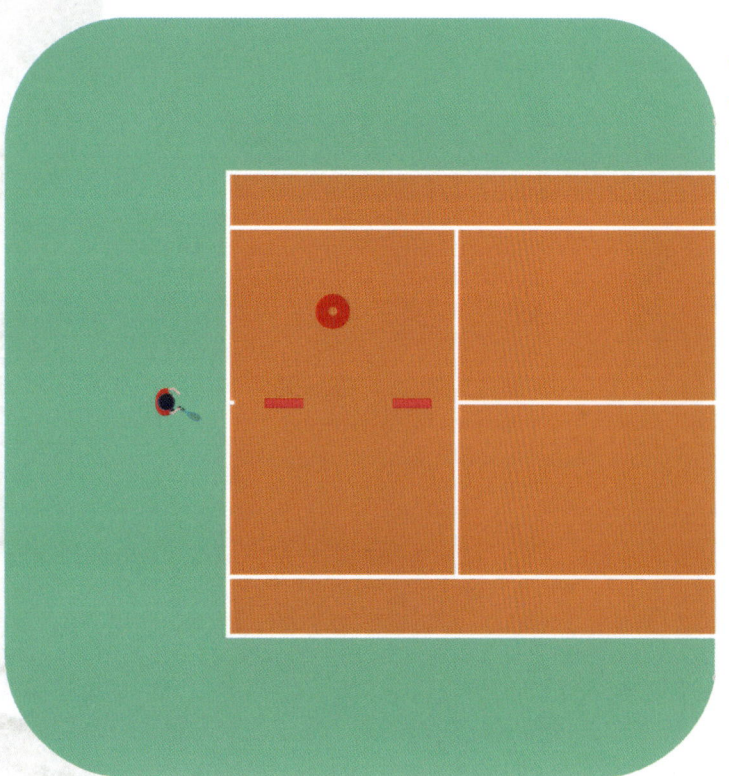

- Minimum 2 players
- Throw down lines
- Cones
- Balls

DIRECTIONS

1. The court is marked out into zones. You can mark out as many or as few zones as you wish, I recommend four. The more zones, the easier the game.
2. Each player can place a cone into one zone - This is where they feel it's dangerous for their opponent to hit into.
3. Players now can't hit the ball into the marked zone.
4. Players play points and lose if they hit the ball onto the marked zone.
5. Players can move the cone after every point.
6. Add more cones into the game as you see fit.

PRISONER

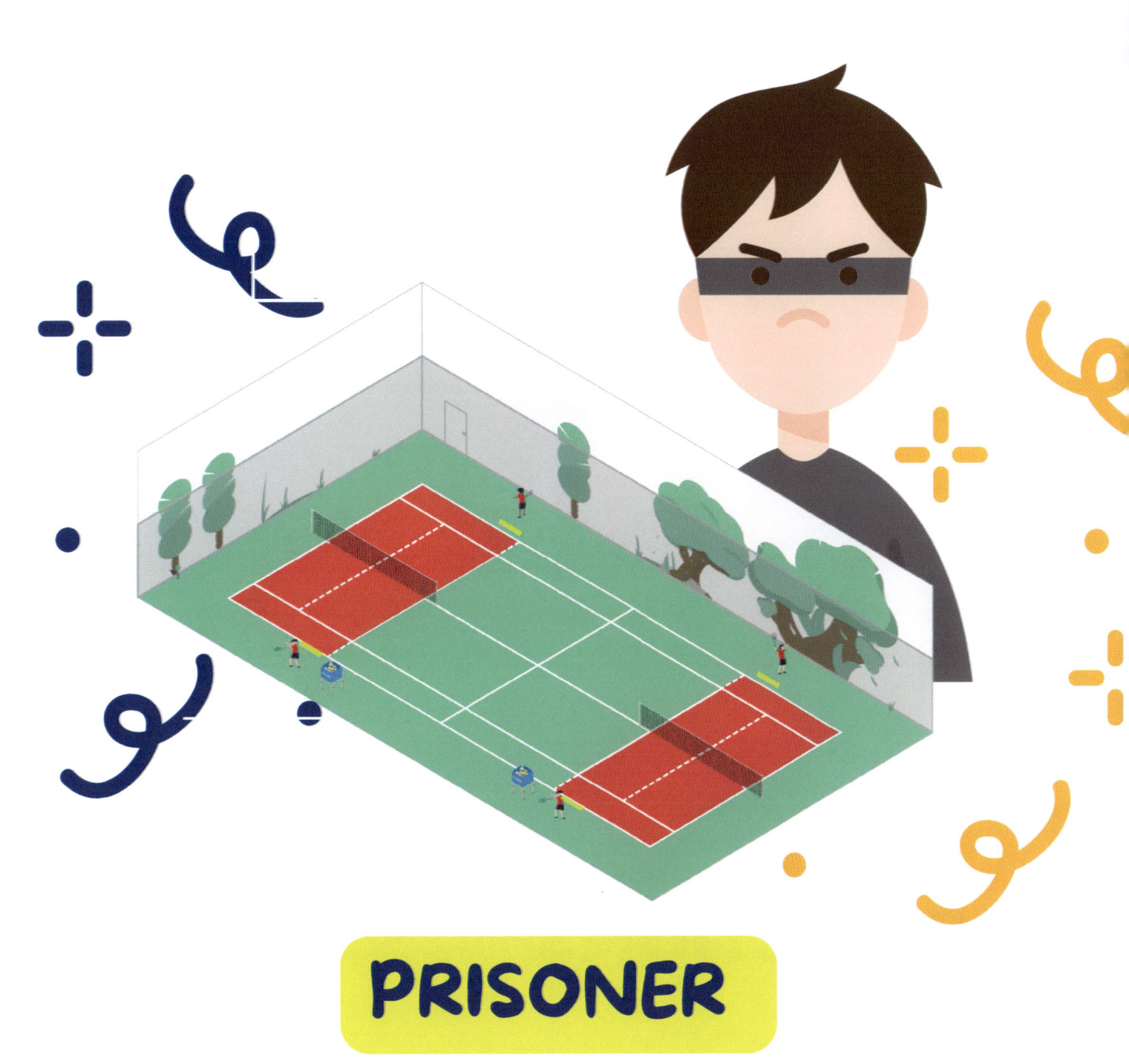

EQUIPMENT

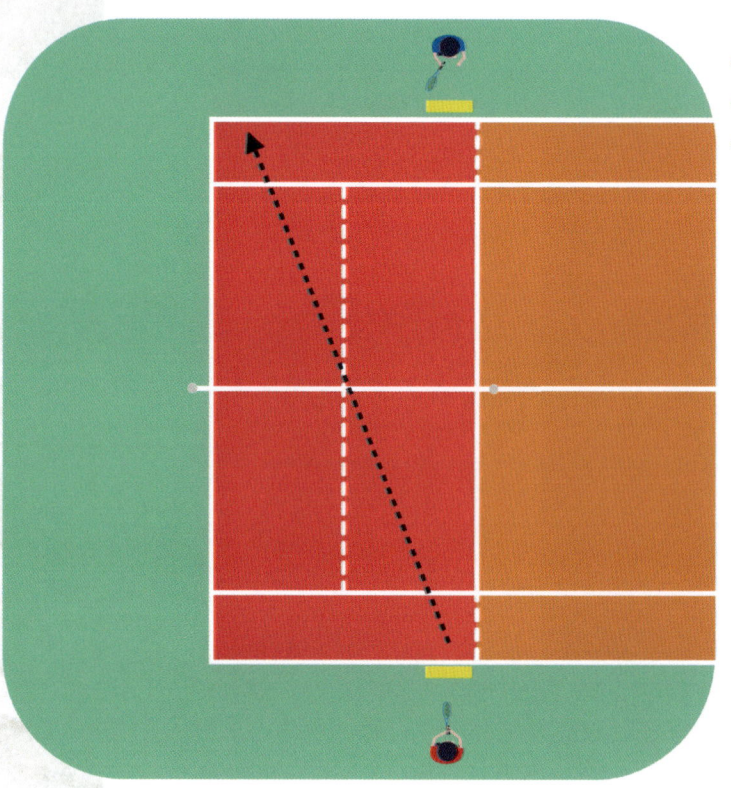

- Minimum two players
- Spots or throw-down lines
- Balls

DIRECTIONS

1. The attacker starts with a ball and stands on a marker in either the forehand or backhand corner.
2. The defender (prisoner) starts in line with the attacker on the opposite baseline.
3. The attacker must throw the ball above head height and hit the ball into the open court.
4. The prisoner can pick up their racket and move when the attacker throws the ball.
5. The prisoner must try and get the ball back.
6. It can be a closed drill (2 shots), or they can play the point out.
7. First to 7 and then rotate.

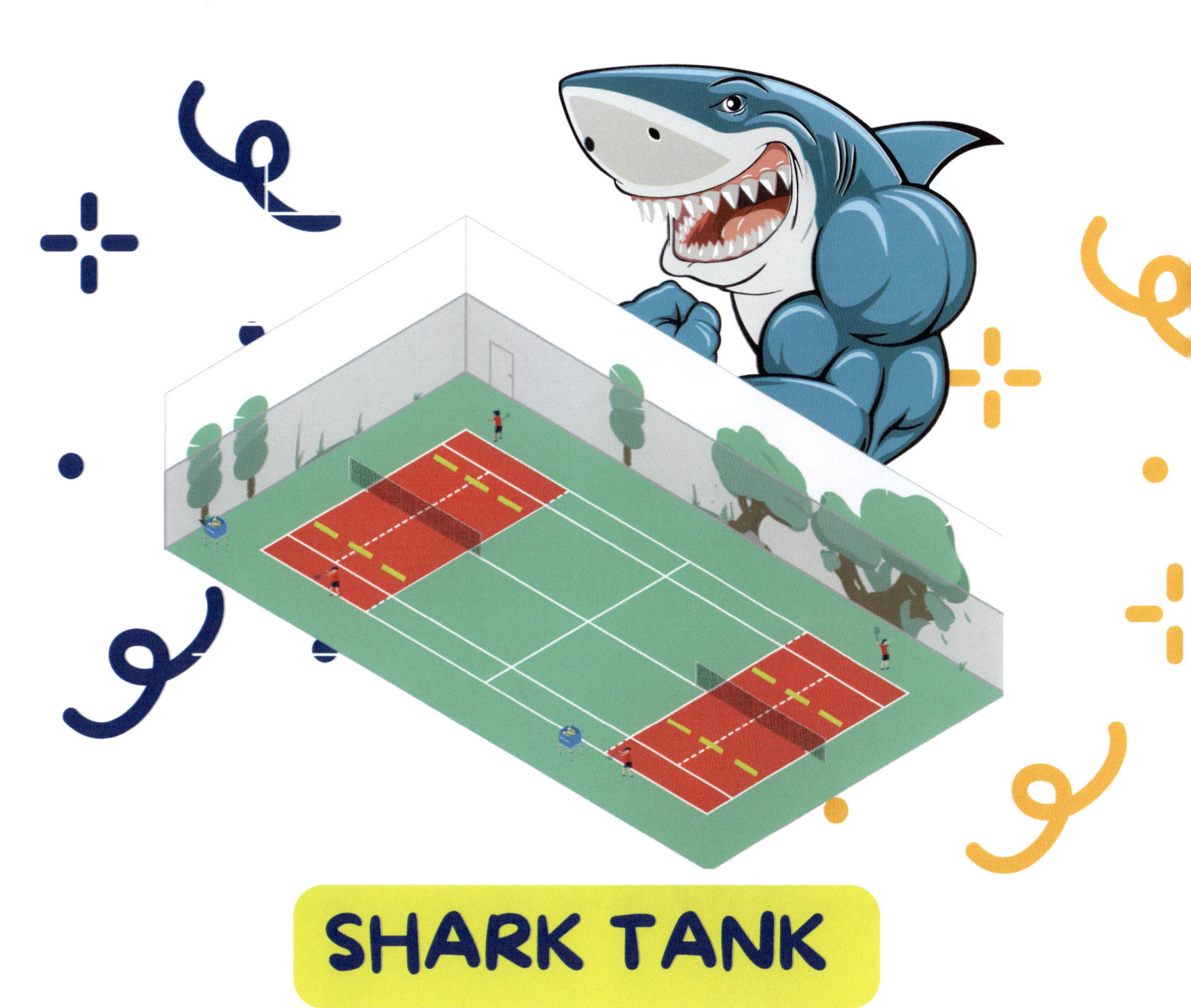

SHARK TANK

EQUIPMENT

- Minimum two players
- Throw down lines or spots
- Balls

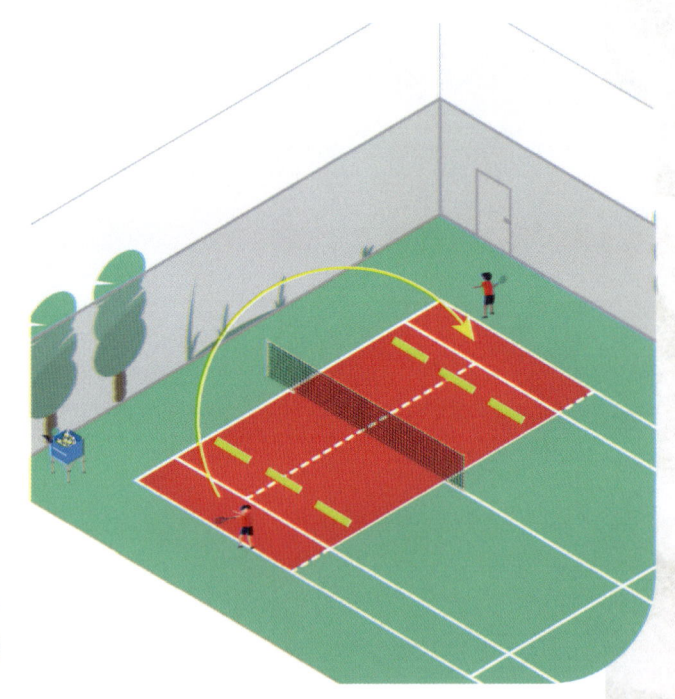

DIRECTIONS

1. Two players mark out the shark tank. The tank must be a challenge for the players. The players lay out the throw-down lines on the court, you may need to help the players set a suitable area.
2. Players take turns to serve to start the rally.
3. Players work together to rally in a both-back situation.
4. The rally aims to keep your partner out of the shark tank.
5. If a player steps into the tank, the rally is over.
6. Players start again and attempt to beat their top score.
7. Play for a set period.

ZOMBIES

EQUIPMENT

- Minimum three players
- Spots to mark out Zombie spaces
- Balls

DIRECTIONS

1. Two Players start the game as the hitters, located at the baseline on either side of the net.
2. The remaining players are Zombies; they sit next to the net on the spot or throw down the line.
3. The two hitters must rally and aim to keep the ball above the zombies.
4. Zombies can use their rackets to attempt to touch the ball; Zombies must stay in a sitting-down position.
5. If a zombie touches the ball, they regain their life and take the place of the hitter who missed.
6. Hitters can also become Zombies if they miss; zombies on their side will take their place.

CHOOSE A SIDE

EQUIPMENT

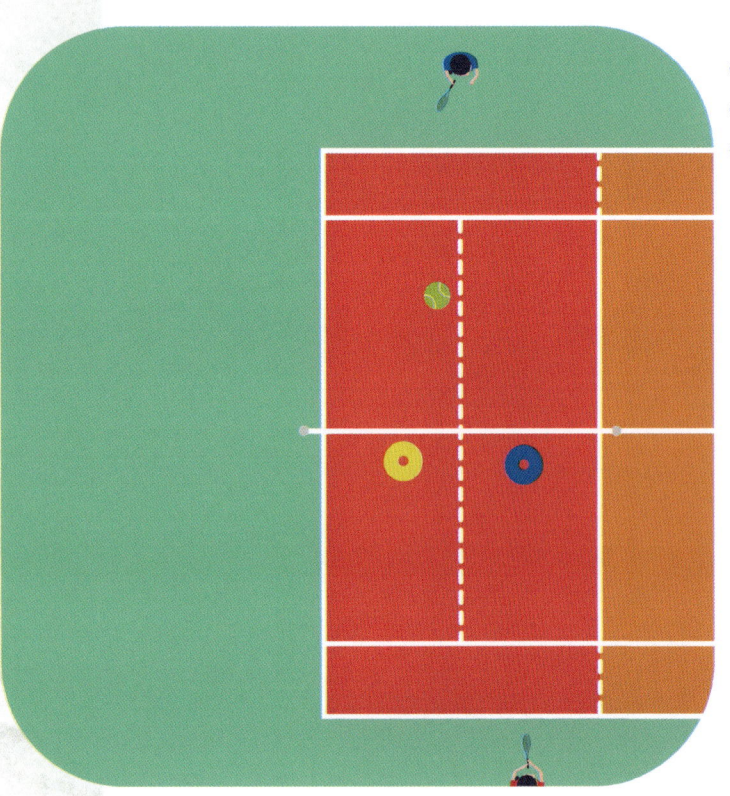

- Minimum two players
- Throw down lines
- Spots

DIRECTIONS

1. Players in pairs.
2. One Player is the attacker, and one player is the defender.
3. Players each choose to stand on the yellow or blue side of the court.
4. The attacker starts with the ball.
5. The attacker can either hit yellow or blue and must decide to attack the space or try and go back behind the defender.
6. The defender must decide to try and cover the space or risk standing wide.
7. Players play to 7 or 10 points and then change roles.

RADICAL RALLIES

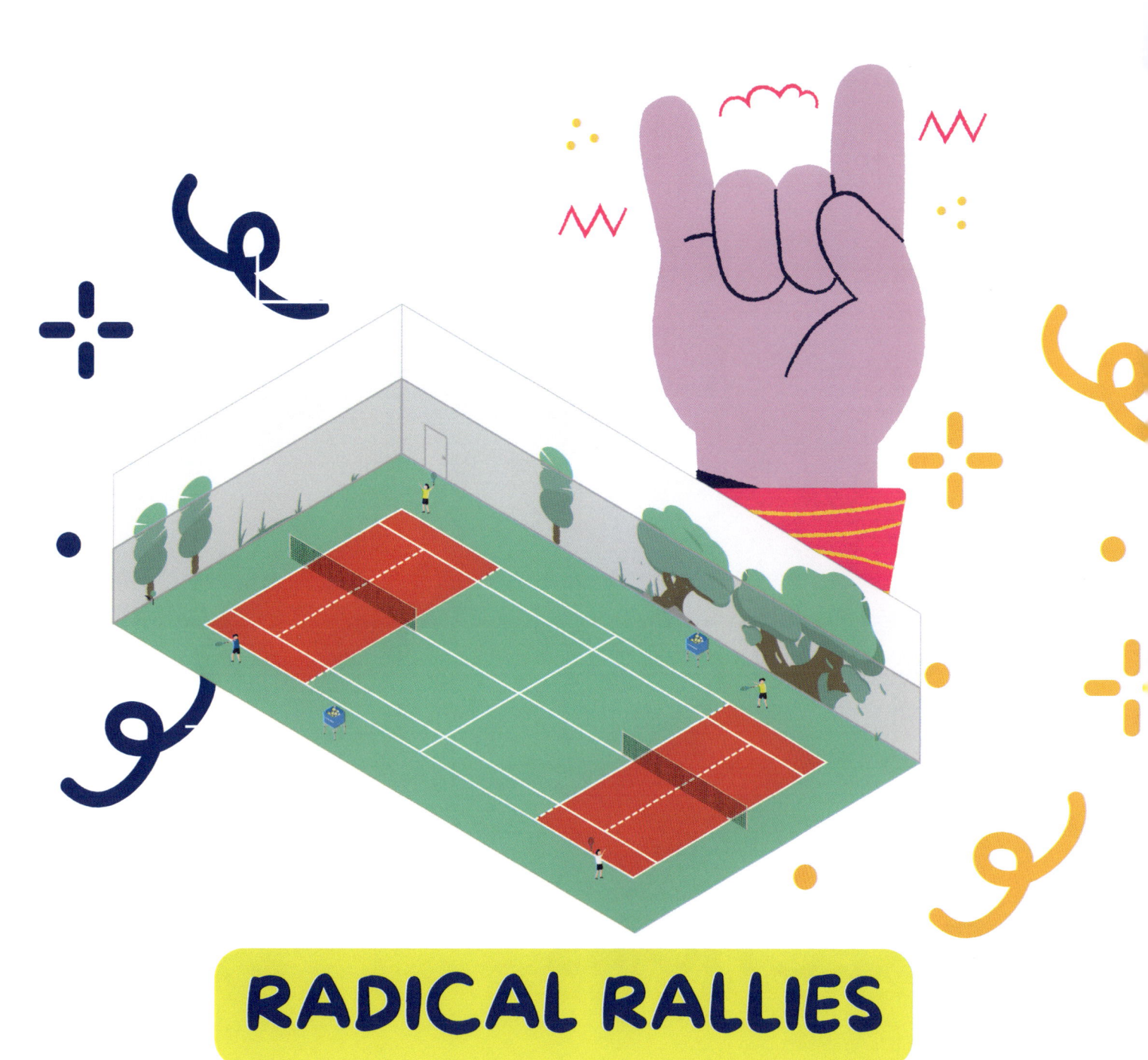

EQUIPMENT

- Minimum two players

DIRECTIONS

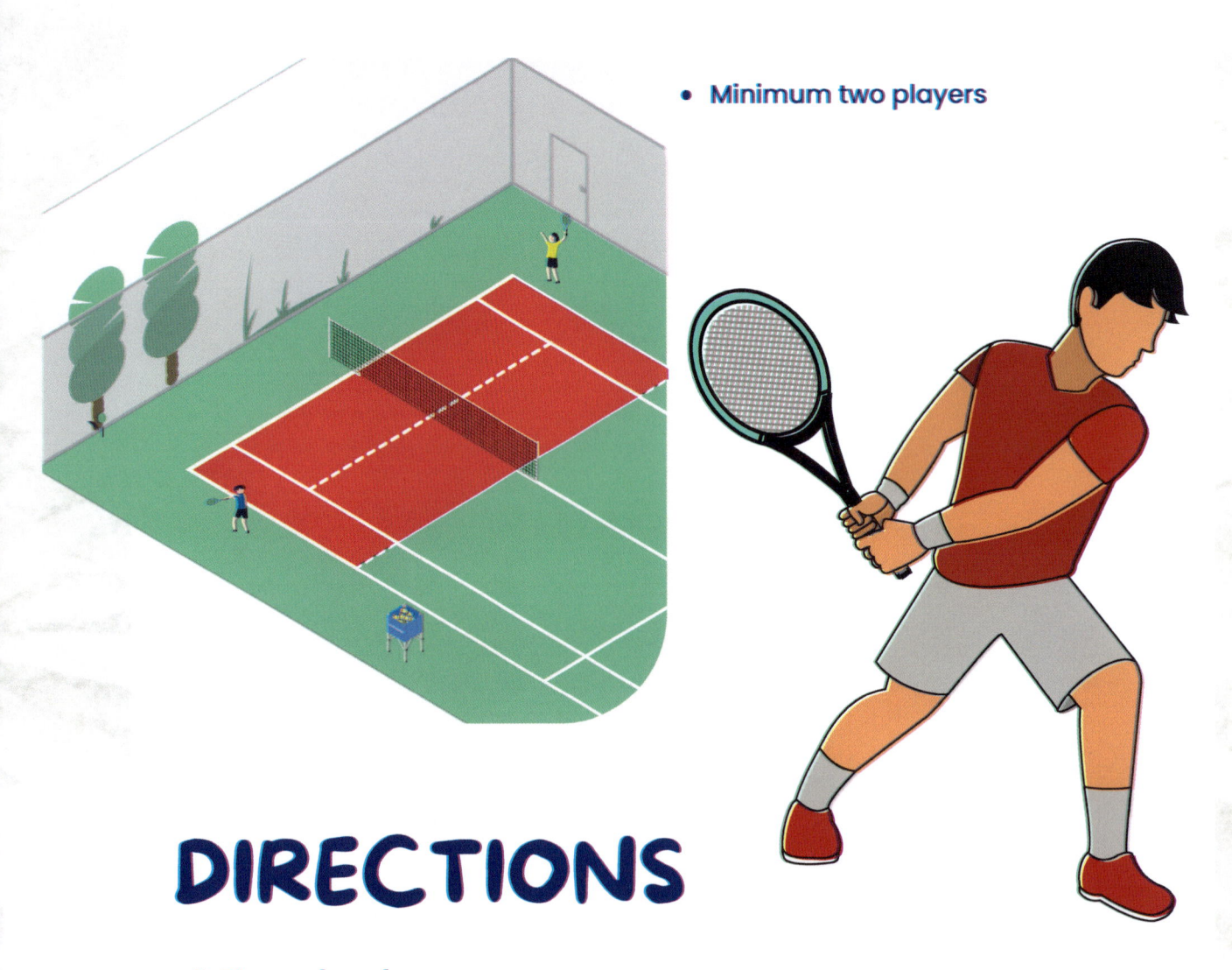

1. Players in pairs.
2. Players rally in pairs; every time the ball lands on the court, it's worth one point. A ten-shot rally is worth ten as an example.
3. When a player misses, their opponent wins the value of the rally, ie a rally to twenty is worth twenty points etc.
4. The first player to 100 points wins the game. (or whatever the coach/player set as the outcome goal)

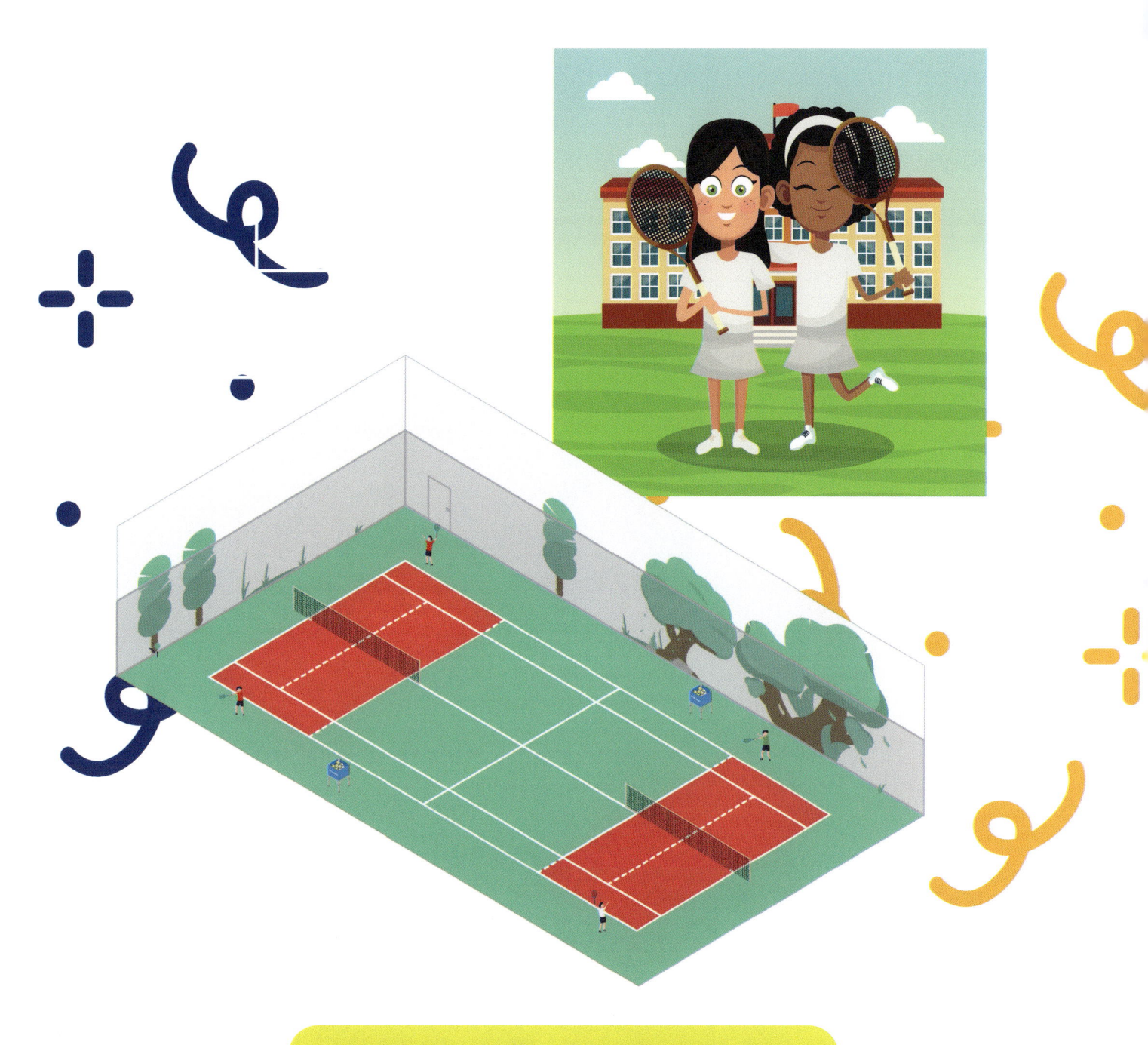

TEAM RALLY

EQUIPMENT

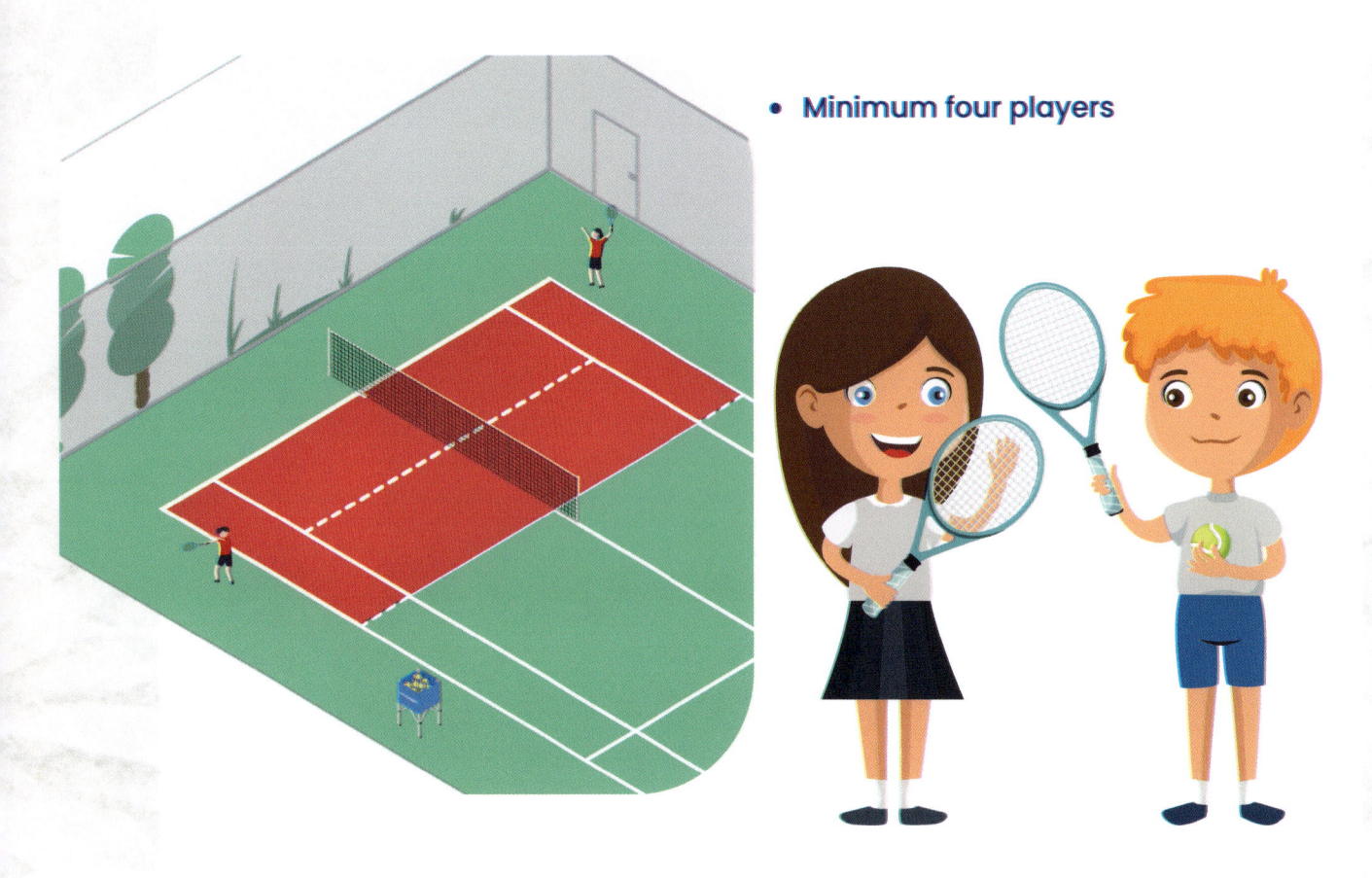

- Minimum four players

DIRECTIONS

1. Players in pairs.
2. The group set a high rally threshold target, i.e. 200, 300, 400.
3. The coach divides the target between the pairs, i.e. 200 between 4 players would be 100 per pair, 200 between 8 players would be 50 per pair.
4. Each pair rallies to its target, i.e. 100 or 50.
5. Every successful shot is worth 1.
6. When an error is made, the players carry on from the score.
7. When each pair reach its target the challenge is complete.
8. When a pair completes their target, they play points against each other until the other pairs complete.

COW

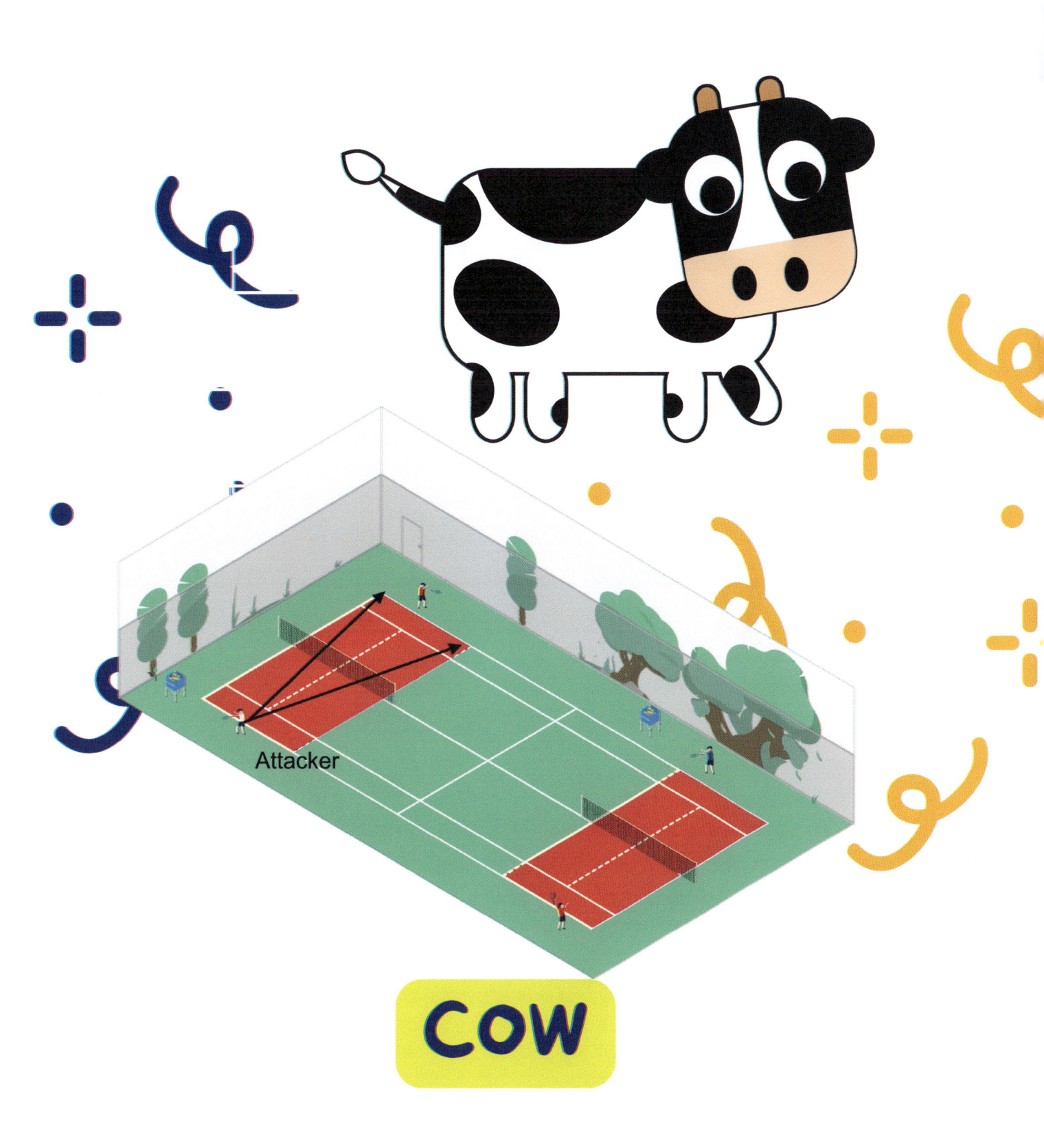

EQUIPMENT

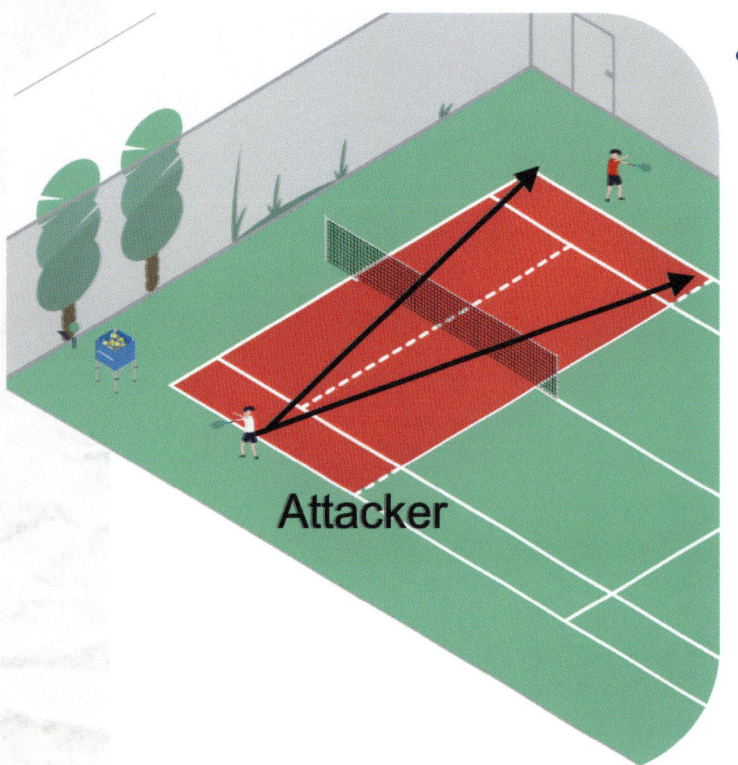

- Minimum two players

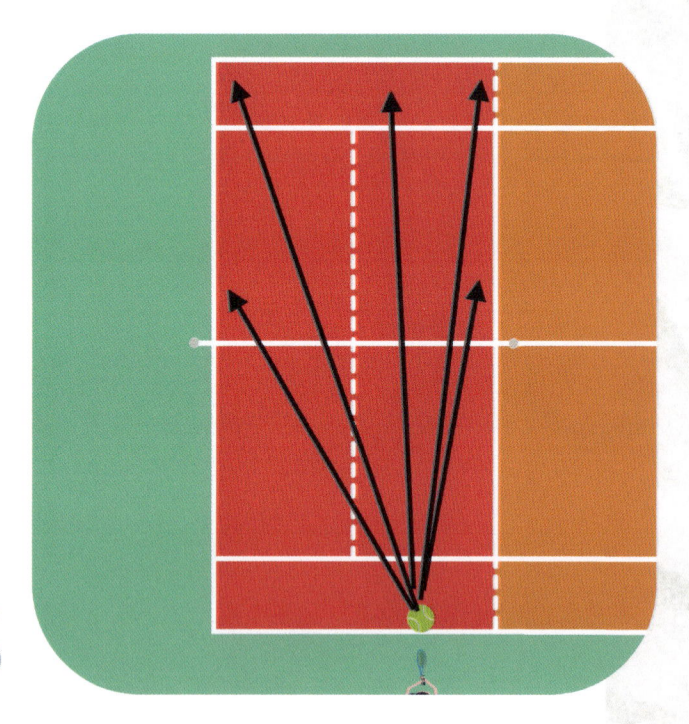

Attacker

DIRECTIONS

1. Players in pairs.
2. One player is the attacker, and one player is the defender.
3. The attacker starts the point with the ball in their hand.
4. They can hit the ball anywhere they want, how they want.
5. The defender has to try and get the ball back.
6. The players can play just two shots, attack and defence, or they can play the point out.
7. First to 7 or ten, and then the players change roles.

GRACE'S HOT POTATO

EQUIPMENT

- Minimum two players

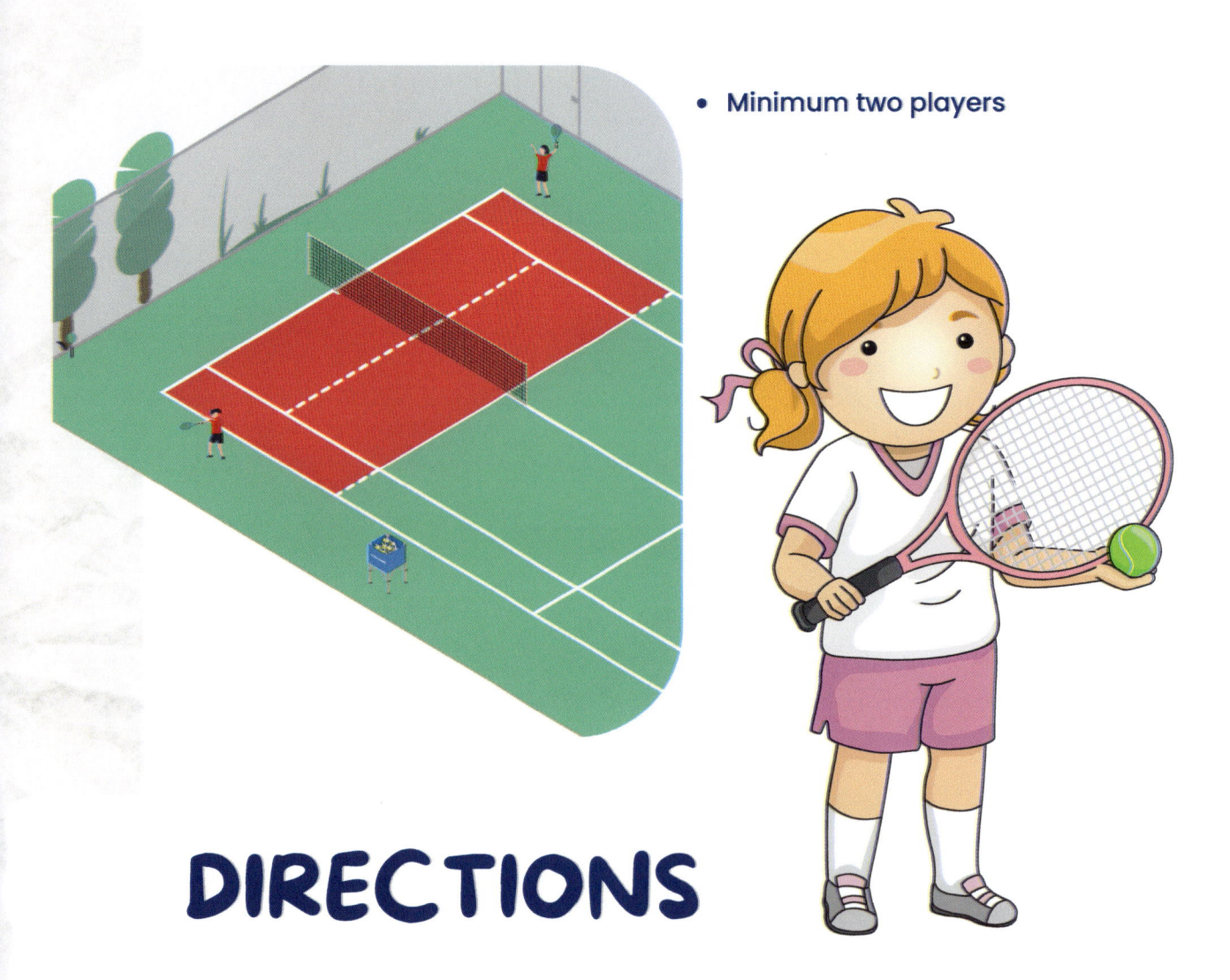

DIRECTIONS

1. Players in pairs.
2. Players rally but, in between, must touch the ball up and catch on their racket.
3. They can then move two steps before dropping the ball and trying to make their opponent miss.
4. The players are not allowed to use their hands.

OVER OR UNDER

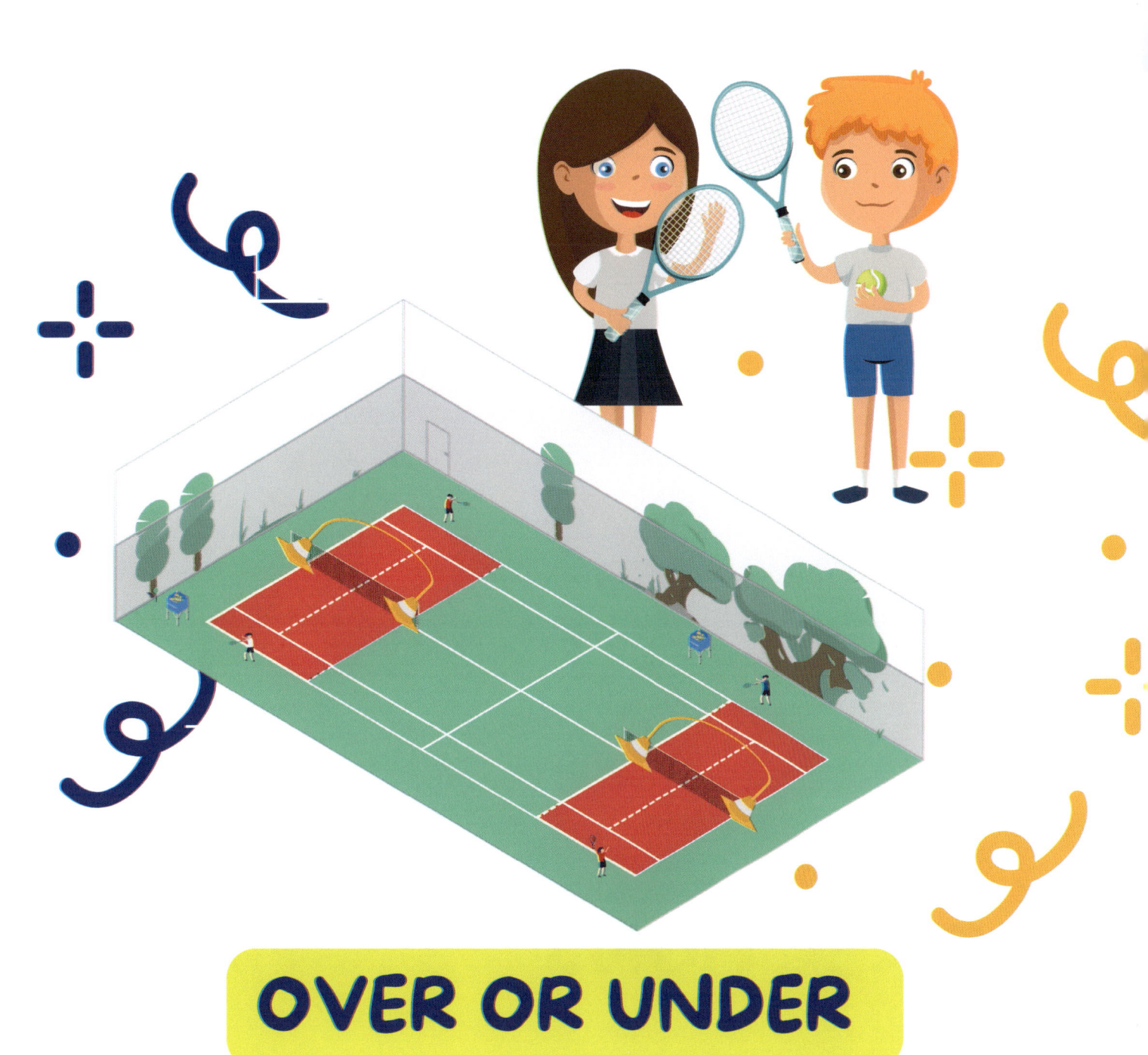

48

EQUIPMENT

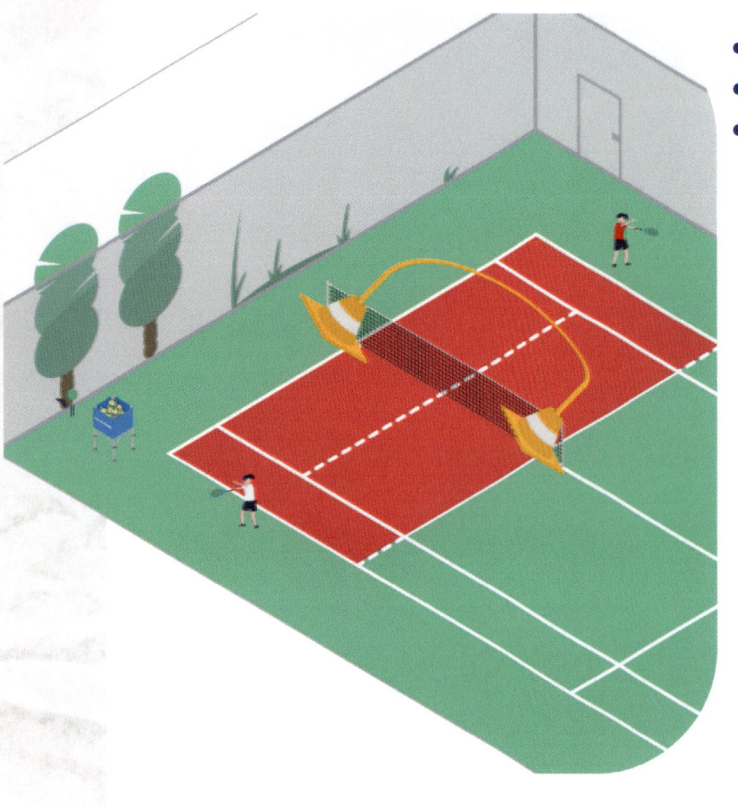

- Minimum two players
- Barrier tape & posts
- Throw down line

DIRECTIONS

1. Players in pairs.
2. Players can either hit the ball over the barrier tape or under.
3. Players score one point if they win by going over the tape.
4. Players score 5 points if they win by going under the barrier tape.
5. The game is designed for players to become aware of hitting a lower flatter ball to try and win the point.
6. Can they find the right time to go low and the right time to go high?

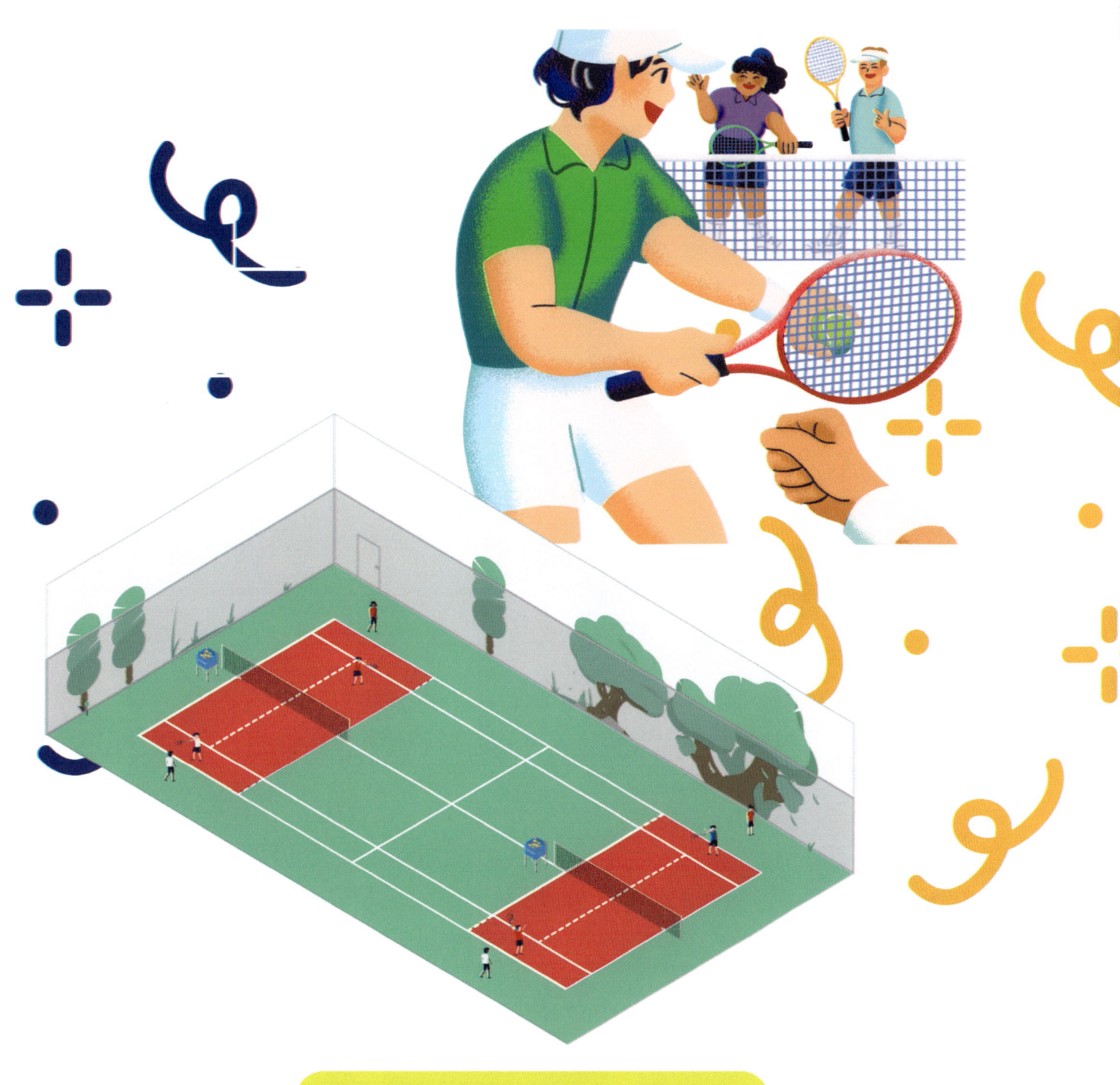

PASS IT ON

50

EQUIPMENT

- Minimum four players

DIRECTIONS

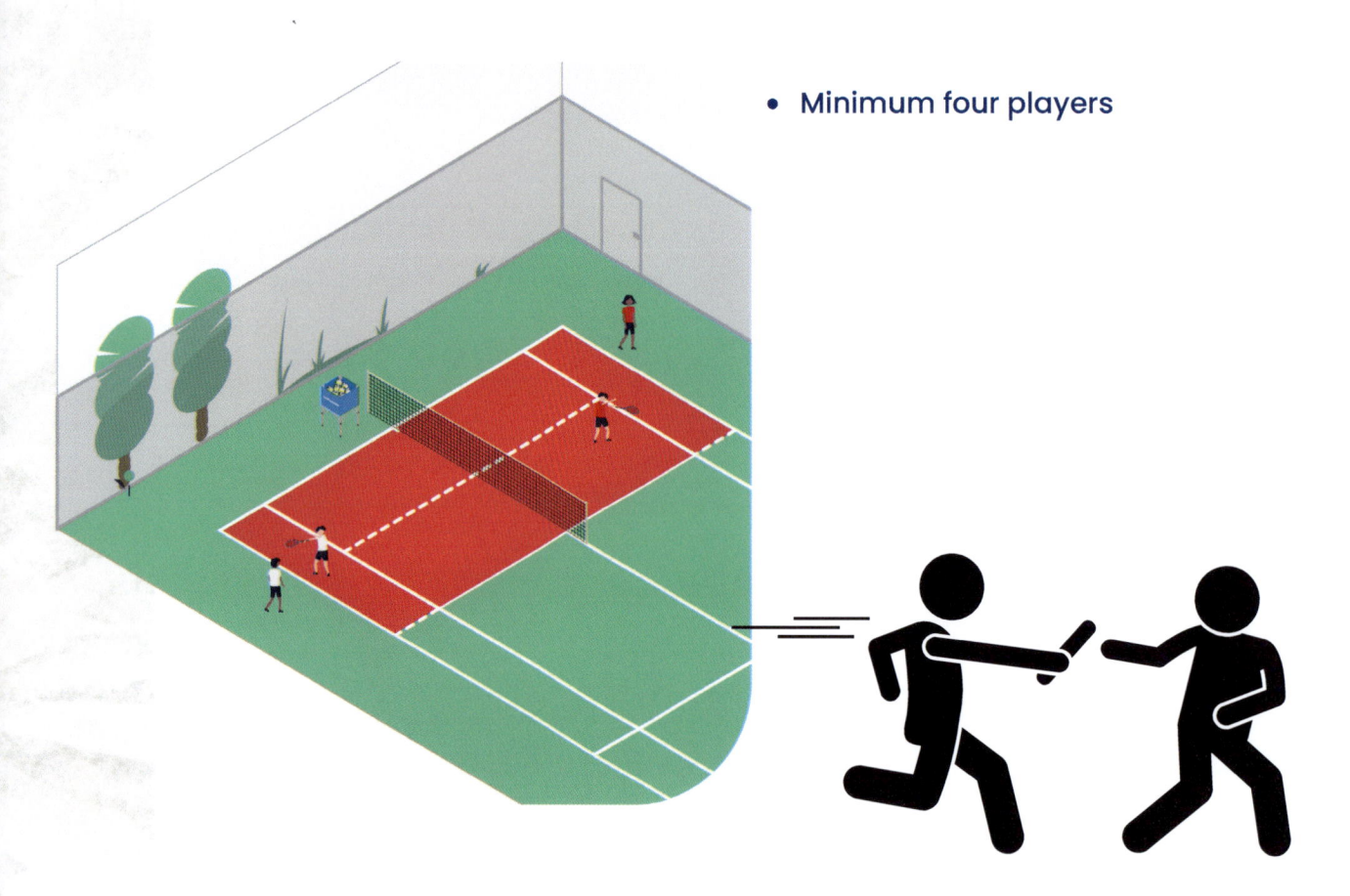

1. Players in pairs with one racket between two.
2. Players number themselves one and two.
3. Player one starts with the racket.
4. Player two stands behind the baseline in a safe position.
5. Player one hits the ball and passes the racket onto player two.
6. The opposite team do the same.
7. Players must learn to control time and space to stay in or win the point.

SWITCH

EQUIPMENT

- Minimum four players
- Two blue spots
- Two red spots
- Throw down lines

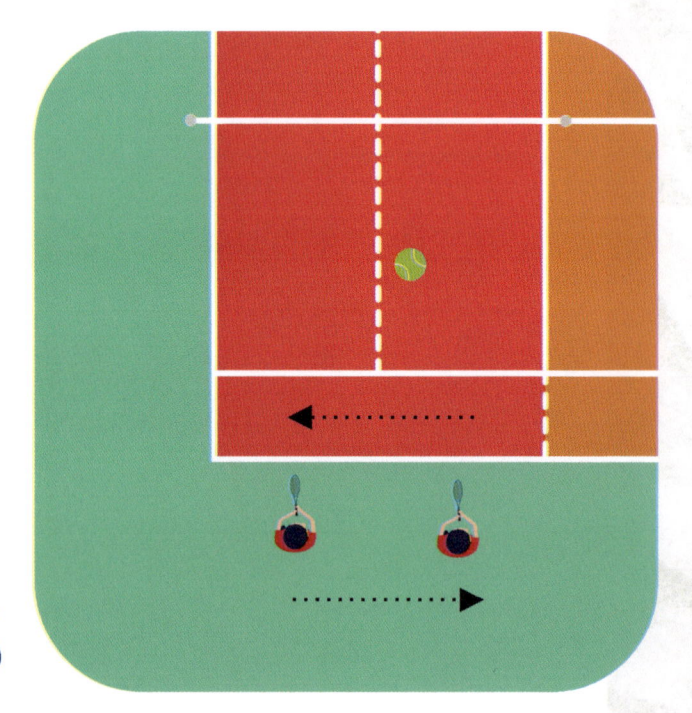

DIRECTIONS

1. Players in pairs, one on the blue side and one on the red side.
2. The opposite teams are set up in the same way.
3. When a team hits the ball, those two players must change positions.
4. When the opposition touches the ball, they must also change positions.
5. Players must work out how to control time to stay or win the point.
6. Play to 7 and change partners.

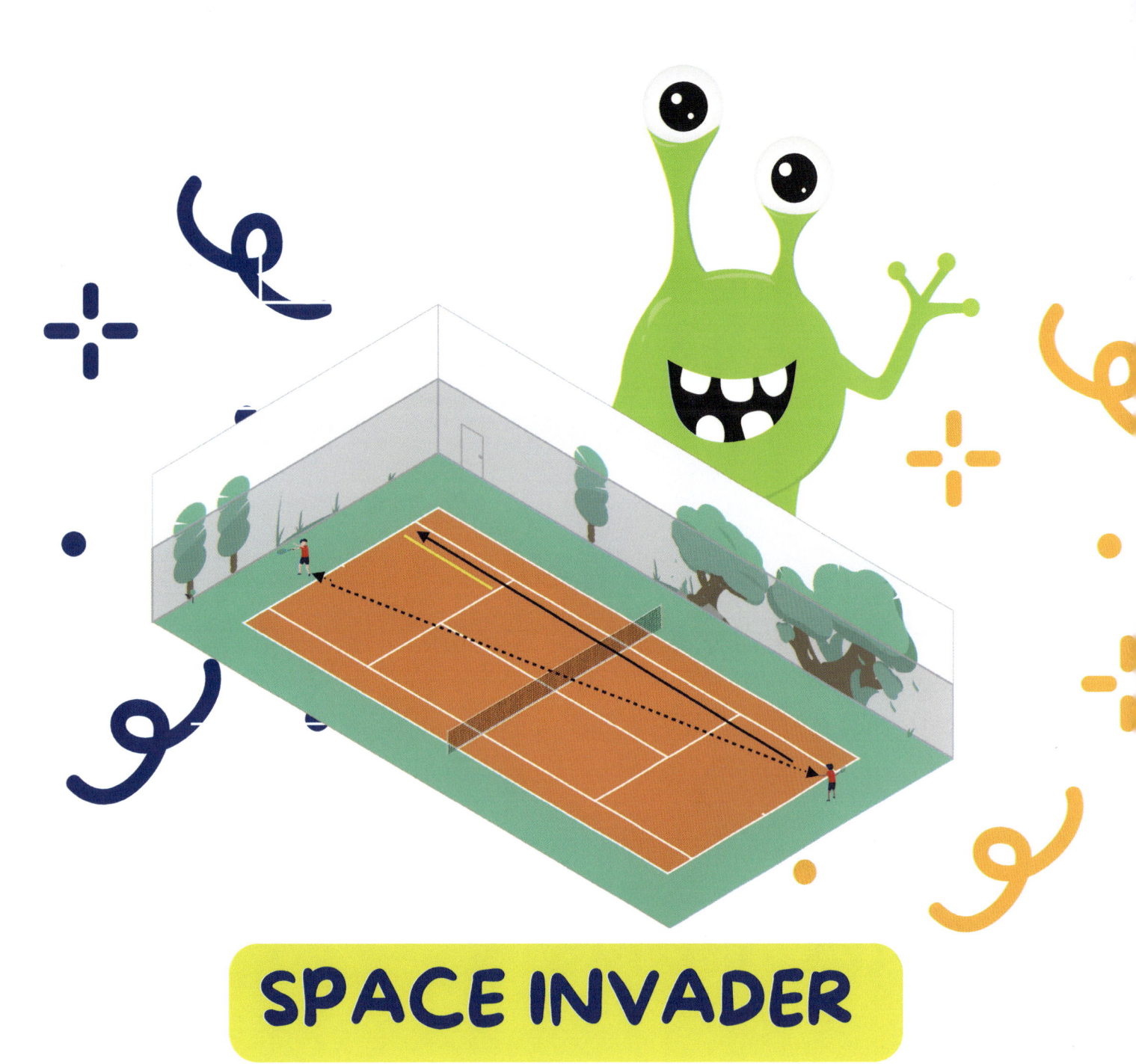

SPACE INVADER

EQUIPMENT

- Minimum two players
- 2 red spots and 2 blue spots
- Throw down line

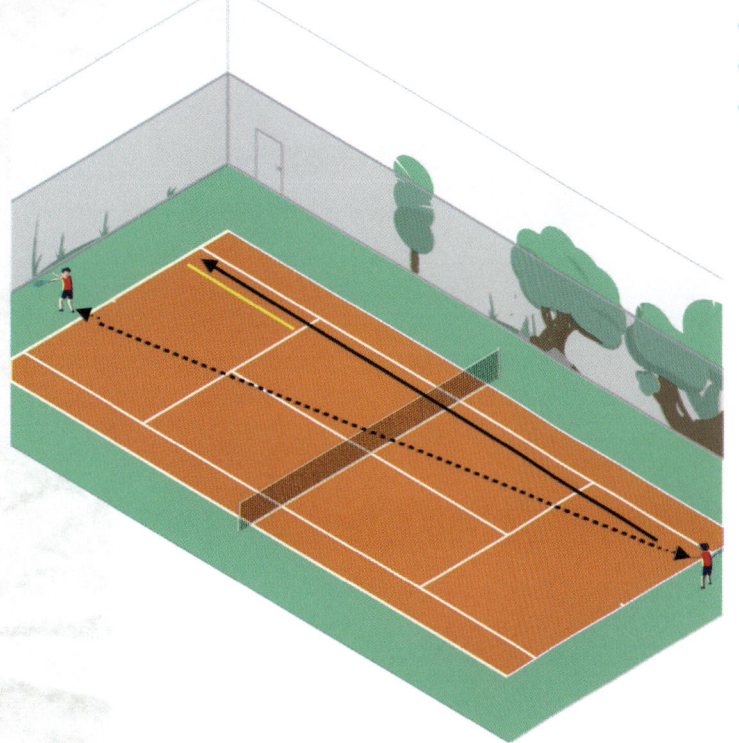

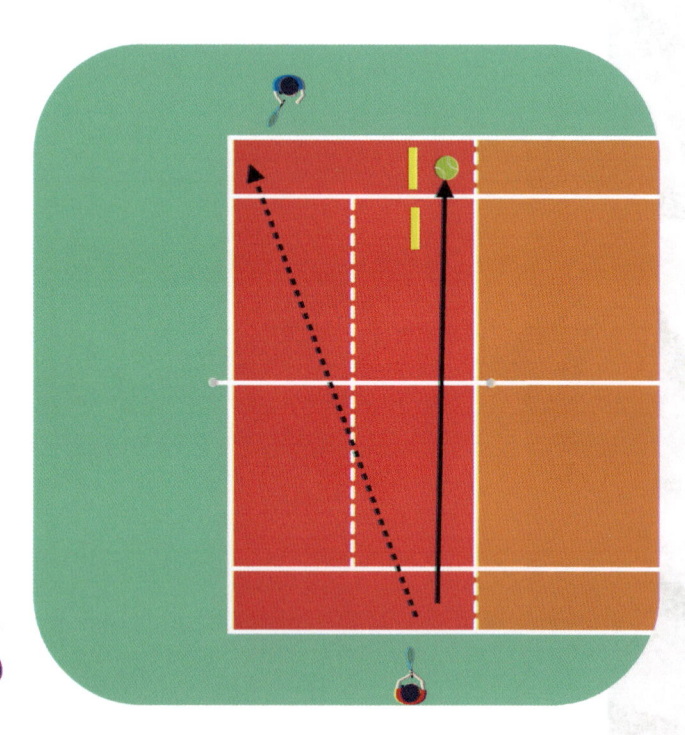

DIRECTIONS

1. Players in pairs, Player A is the space invader, and Player B is the defender.
2. Players A and B rally cross court.
3. Player A decides when to change direction and hit down the line.
4. The point is live when the direction is changed.
5. To upskill this game, player A may set down a target zone. They must hit the zone when they change direction. Otherwise, they lose the point.
6. Play to 7 points and then change roles.
7. Play a further 7 points and change to opposite side.

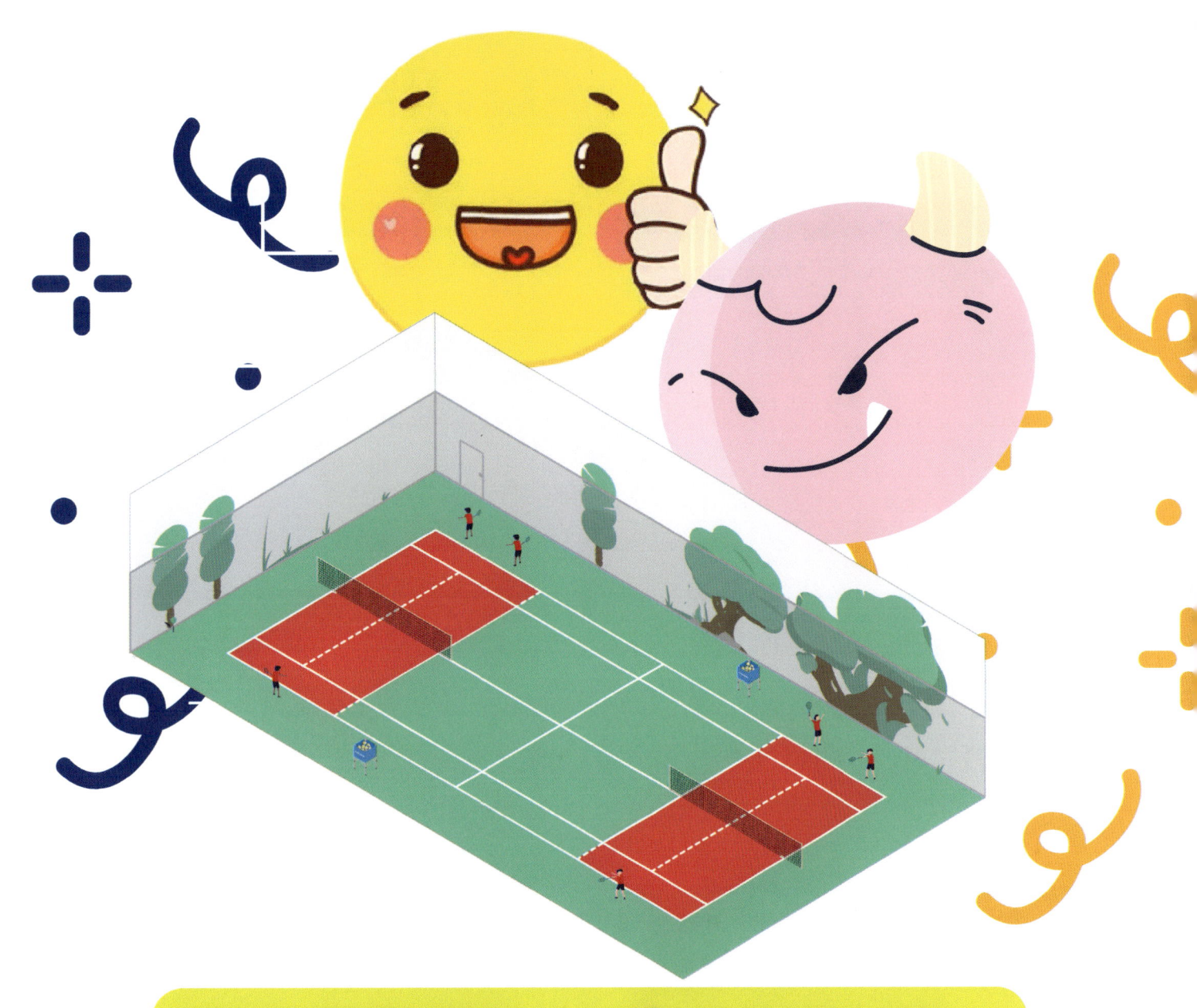

GOODIES V BADDIES

EQUIPMENT

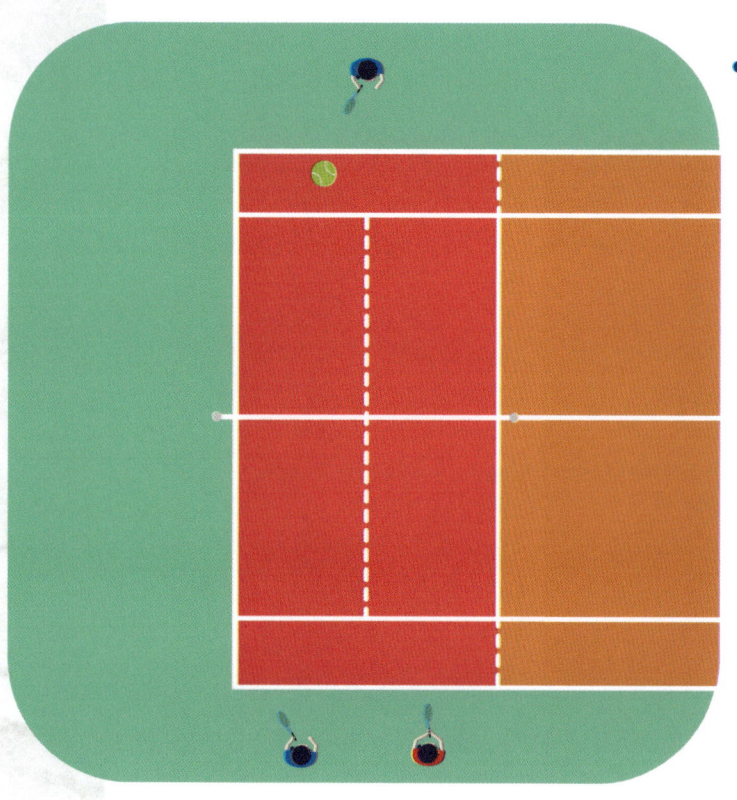

- Minimum 3 players

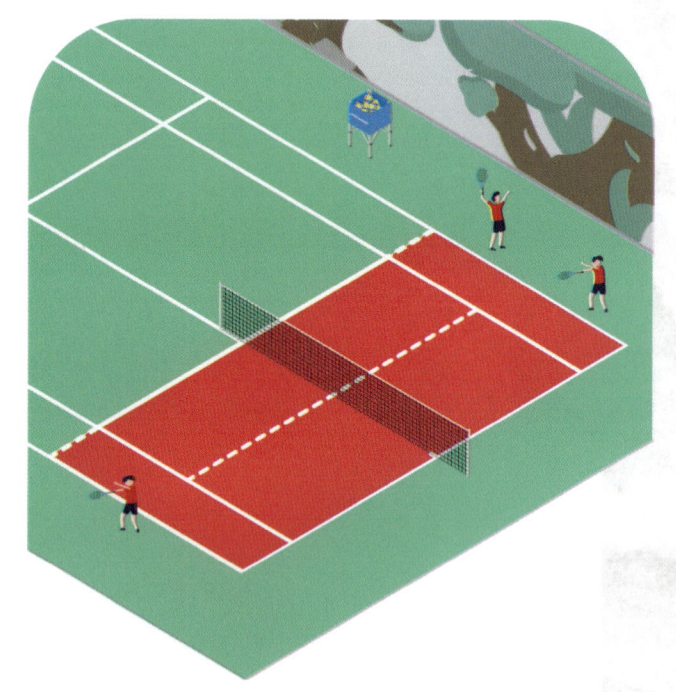

DIRECTIONS

1. Players work in 3's.
2. Two players start on one baseline, the single player opposite on the other.
3. The Single player will hit for 2 minutes, the two players are feeders, and their job is to keep the ball in play.
4. Every time players get the ball in, they score a point, a goodie. Every time they don't, they get a baddie.
5. At the end of 2 minutes, the player takes the baddies away from the goodies and is left with a final score.
6. Rotate players and give each player three attempts to set their highest score.

BACKHAND ONLY

EQUIPMENT

- Minimum two players

DIRECTIONS

1. Players are in pairs.
2. Players can only send back using a backhand.
3. They are allowed as many touches of the ball as they wish, i.e. control with a forehand and switch the ball across the body to the backhand.
4. Players aim to get the ball under control until they feel confident about hitting a backhand.
5. They attempt to send the ball over the net with a backhand when they feel confident.
6. If they succeed, the rally will continue.
7. If they miss, they lose the point.

WHEN SERVING OR RETURNING

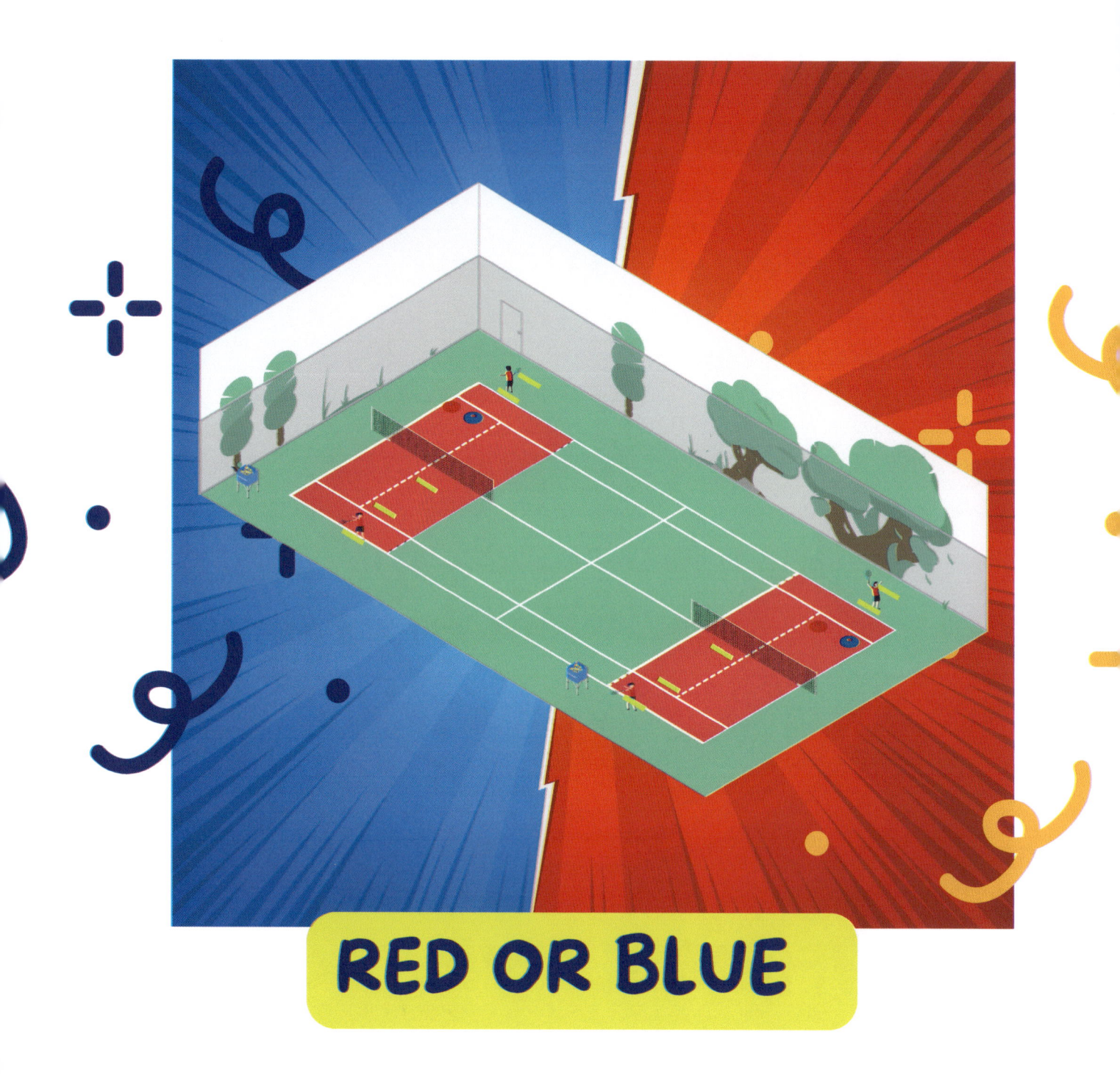

RED OR BLUE

EQUIPMENT

- Minimum two players
- 2 different colour cones (red & blue)
- 5 throw down lines or spots

DIRECTIONS

1. The server decides to start from three positions. (Easy, Normal or Challenging) The server places three throw-down lines in the three areas.
2. The returner places two lines down in an attack (closer) or defence position. (further back position)
3. The server must pick a target area, Red or Blue.
4. The server hits the serve, and if the ball lands in the correct area, they score a point.
5. If the returner gets the ball back, they gain a point.
6. If the returner misses the return, the server receives an additional point.
7. Play to 10 points and then rotate players.

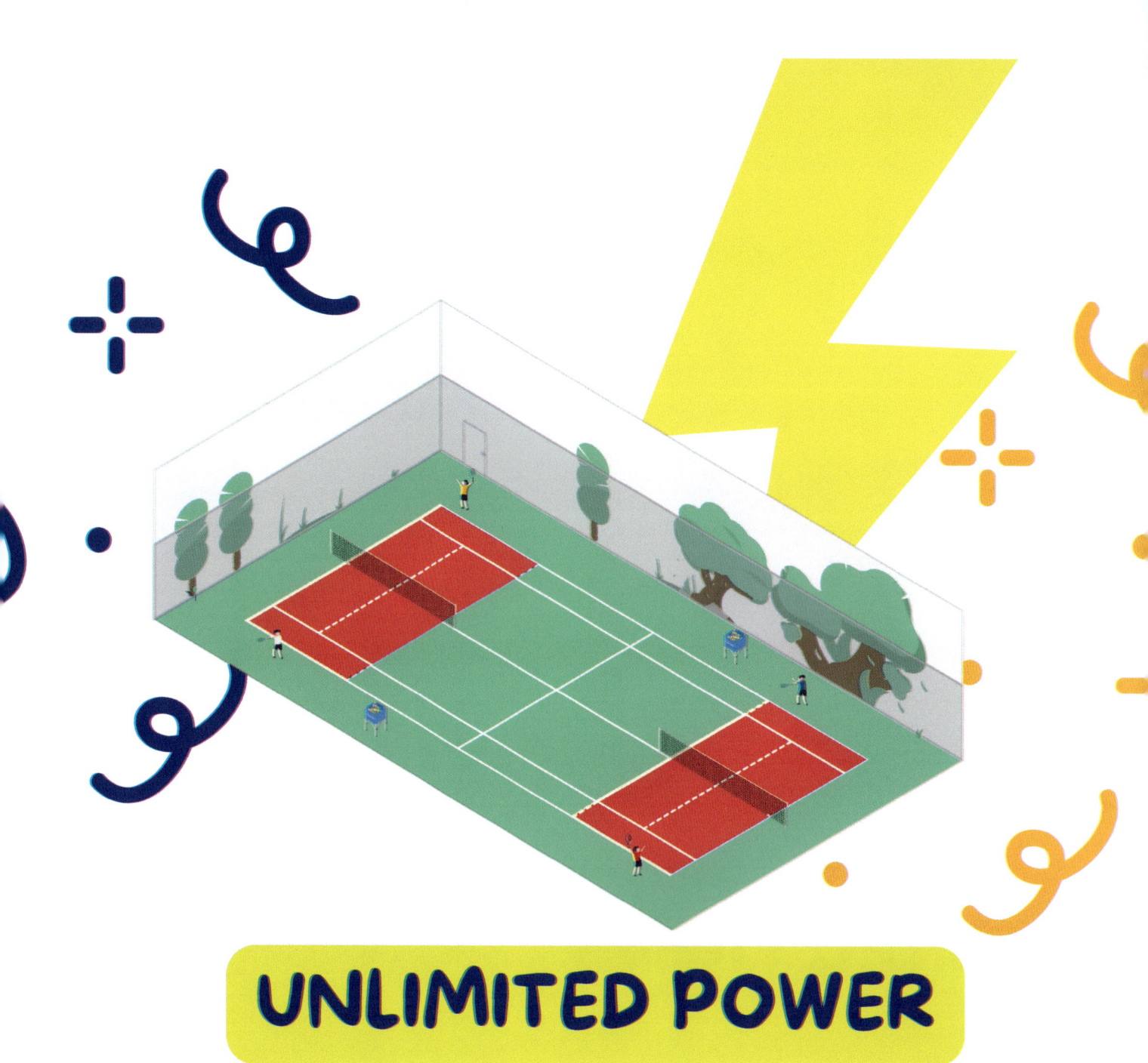

UNLIMITED POWER

EQUIPMENT

- Minimum two players

DIRECTIONS

1. One Player is the server, and the other is the returner.
2. The server has an unlimited number of serves.
3. Once the service goes in, the players rally the point out.
4. Players rotate roles after two points.

NO BOUNDARIES

EQUIPMENT

- Minimum two players

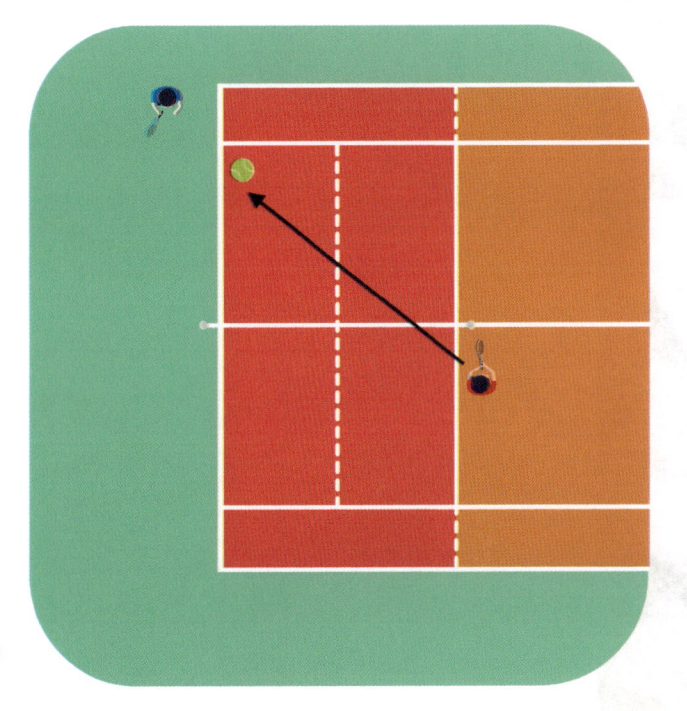

DIRECTIONS

1. Players in pairs.
2. One Player is the server.
3. One Player is the returner.
4. The server can stand anywhere on the court.
5. The returner can also stand anywhere.
6. The server must nominate which service box they are aiming for.
7. Returner must attempt to get the ball back.
8. First to 7 and rotate players around.

REVERSE POWER

EQUIPMENT

- Minimum two players

DIRECTIONS

1. Players in pairs.
2. One server and one returner.
3. Returner calls out where the server must hit, red or blue. (forehand or backhand)
4. Returner decides to try and use their strengths or find a weakness in the server's ability to get direction.

4

CONNECT 4

EQUIPMENT

- Minimum two players
- Sponge balls
- Throw down lines
- Cones

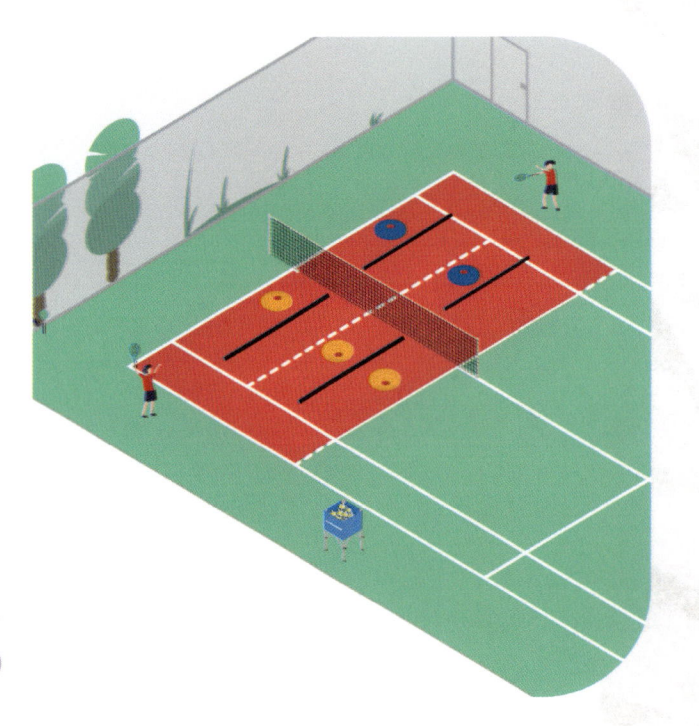

DIRECTIONS

1. Mark out four zones; you can make it even or vary the size of each zone.
2. The server can serve in any of the four zones and stand where they want to behind the baseline.
3. Returners can stand anywhere they wish.
4. The server attempts to serve in one of the four zones. If successful, they get a token. The token is placed into the same zone as the ball landed.
5. The returner attempts to return the serve into one of the opposite four zones. If they are successful, they also get a token.
6. If either player hits the same zone again, they don't score.
7. Who can connect four first?

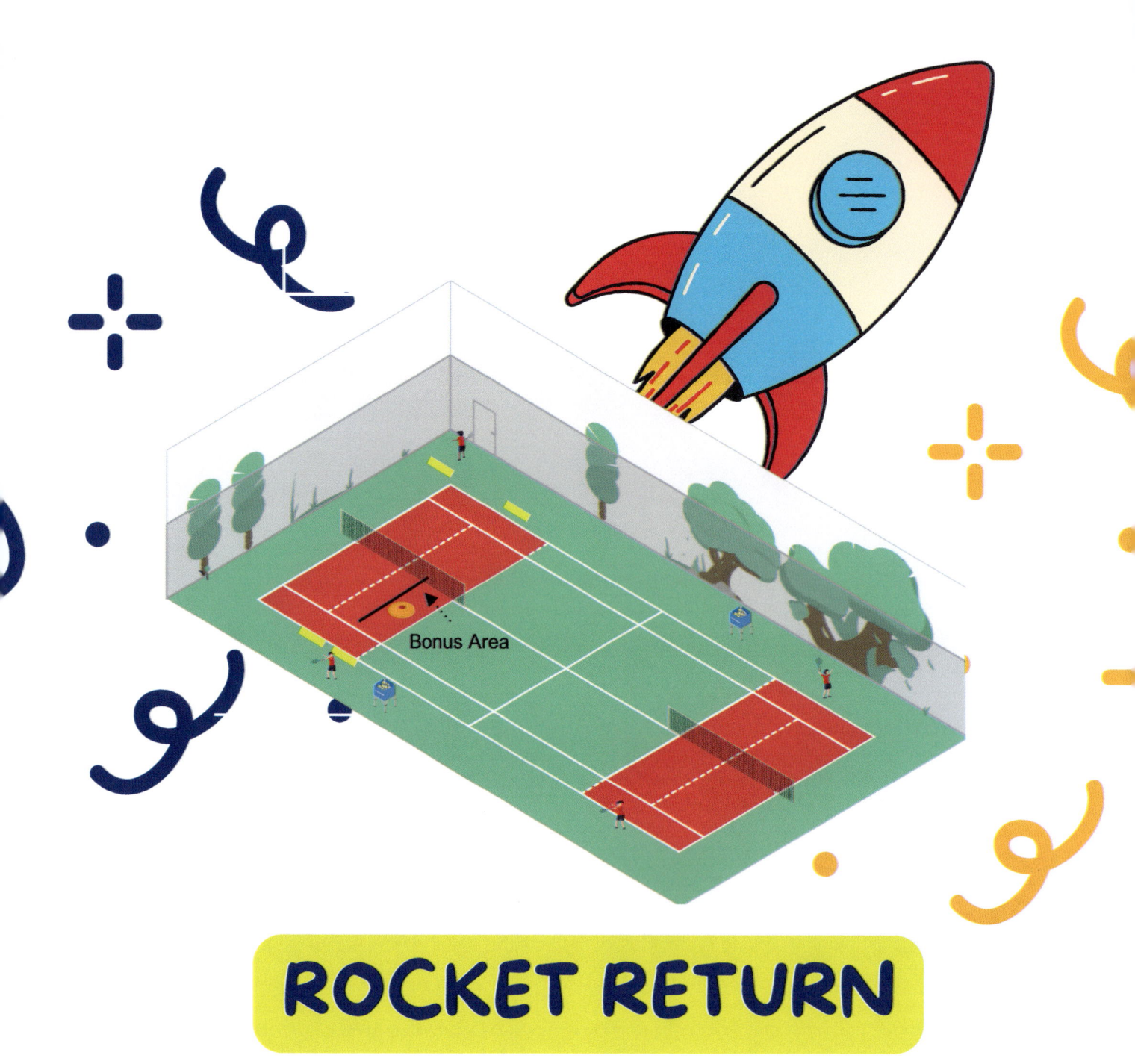

Bonus Area

ROCKET RETURN

EQUIPMENT

- Minimum two players
- Throw down lines & spots

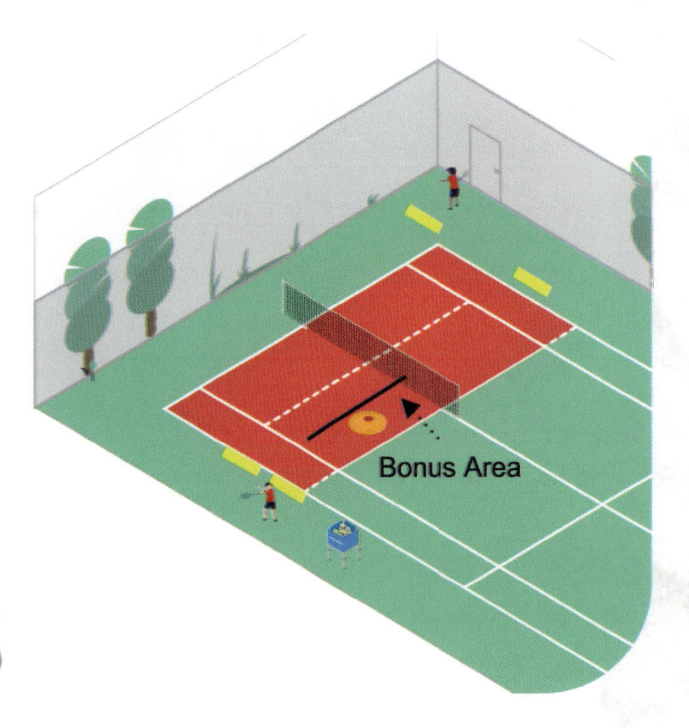

DIRECTIONS

1. The server picks two serving positions, wide and central.
2. Returner sets to starting positions wide and centre - These must be challenging starting positions.
3. A bonus area is marked out for a wide return.
4. The server hits serve into the open service box, and they are trying to make the returner miss.
5. The returner is frozen until the server throws the ball up. They can then move and attempt to get a return back.
6. If the returner hits the ball back, they score. If they miss, the server scores.
7. If the returner hits the ball into the bonus area - they score a bonus point.
8. The first player to 10 and then rotate.

SERVING TORNADO

EQUIPMENT

- Minimum two players
- Hoop

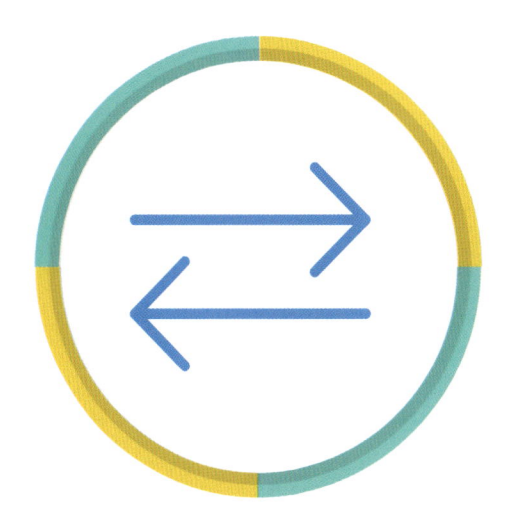

DIRECTIONS

1. Players rally to 4 shots.
2. When they get to 4, one player sets off the tornado.
3. The tornado is a hoop, and the player spins the hoop.
4. Player A is the server, and they try to hit as many shots into the tornado as possible until it stops spinning.
5. Players rally to 4 again. This time the other player serves with player A, spinning the tornado.

NET PLAY

'SMASH IT'

EQUIPMENT

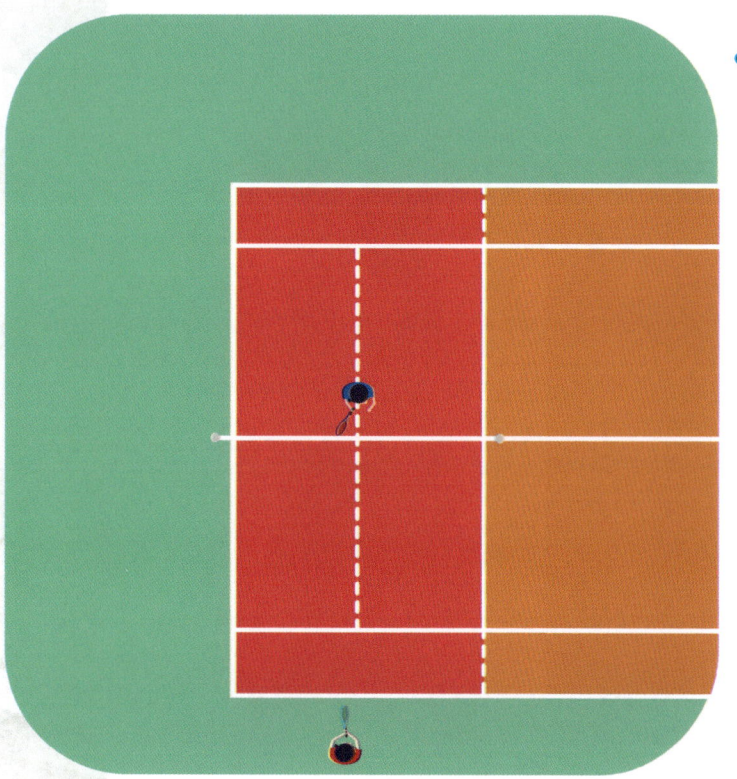

- Minimum two players

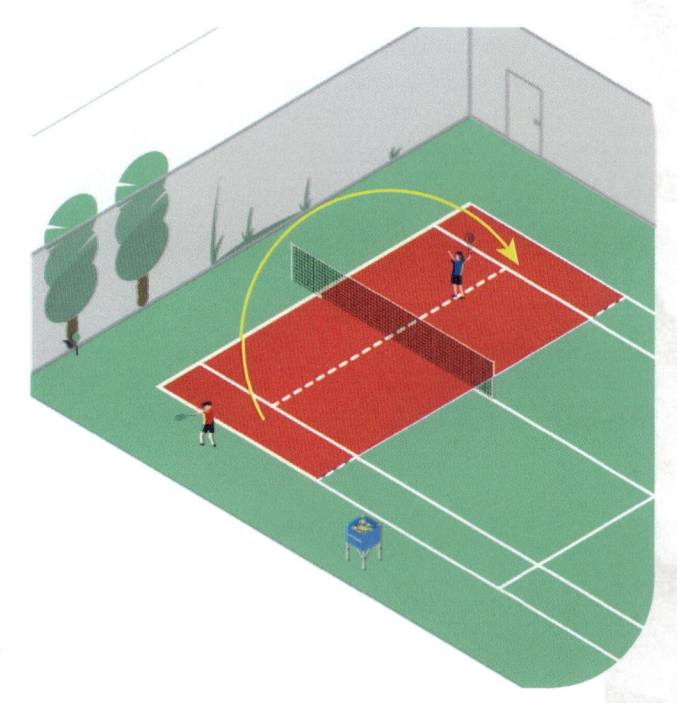

DIRECTIONS

1. A player starts at the net (Attacker), and one player starts at the baseline. (Defender)
2. Defender begins with a ball; they must hit the ball over the head of the attacker.
3. The attacker must move back and control the ball with the racket before or after a bounce so they can then catch it.
4. The attacker is now frozen and can't move their feet.
5. The attacker now throws the ball up and hits a serve / self-feed smash; they attempt to beat the defender.
6. The defender tries to get the ball back.
7. If the defender misses, the attacker wins.
8. If the defender misses, then the attacker wins.

KEEPERS!

EQUIPMENT

- Minimum two players
- Spots
- Throw down lines
- Barrier tape (optional)

DIRECTIONS

1. Players in pairs.
2. Player A is the Tennis Goal Keeper, and they are positioned at the net.
3. Player B is the striker, and they are positioned at the baseline.
4. Player B must try and score by hitting the ball past the goalkeeper and keep the ball out by hitting volleys.
5. The striker is not allowed to lob the goalkeeper, or you can use barrier tape to set up a crossbar.
6. Play first to seven and switch roles.

KEEP IT UP

80

EQUIPMENT

- Minimum two players

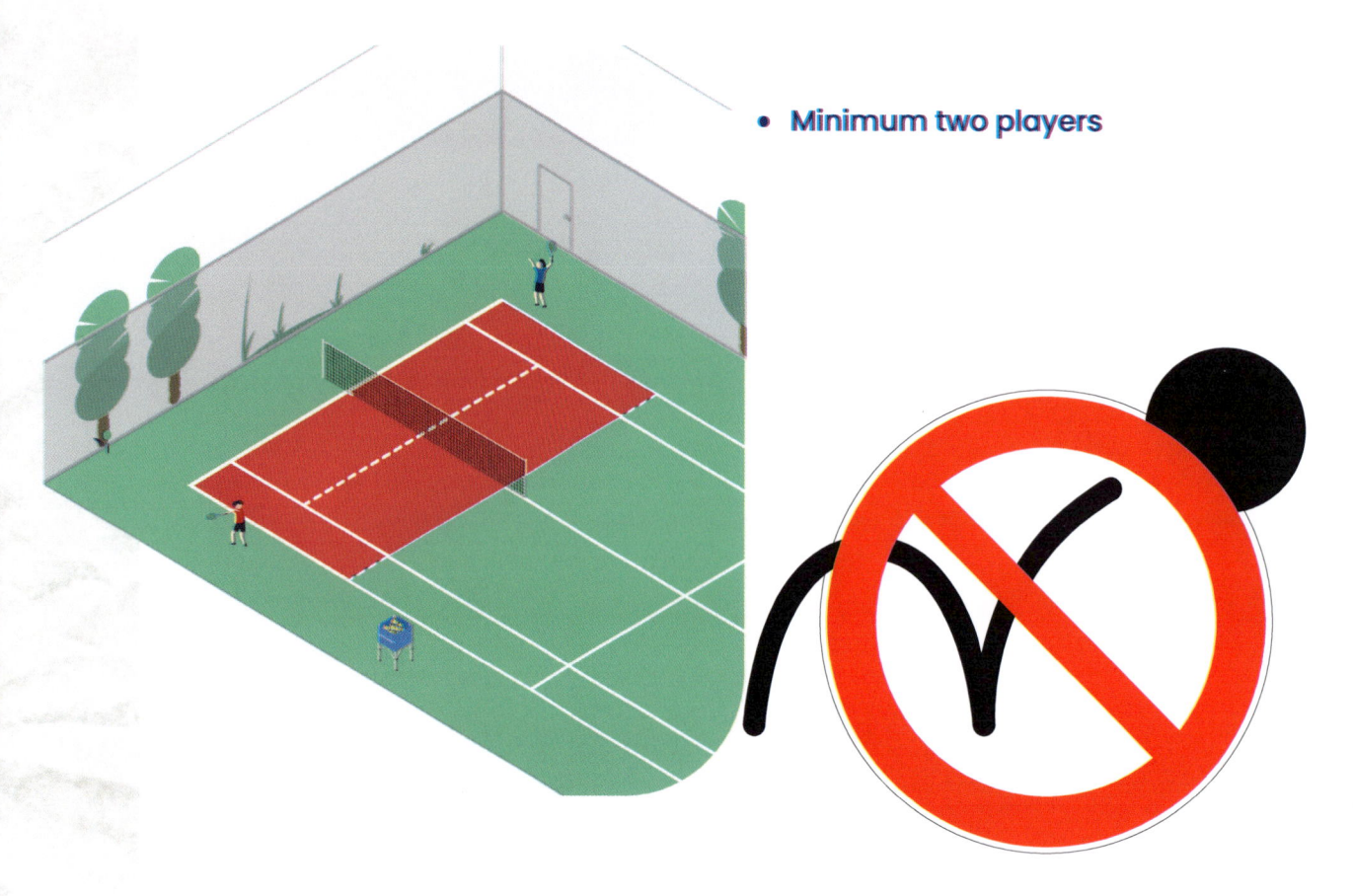

DIRECTIONS

1. Players in pairs.
2. Player A serves player B who hits the return.
3. After the return, the players can't let the ball bounce; they must keep it in the air.
4. Play first to seven and switch roles.

COMPETITIONS

JOKERS TIEBREAK

EQUIPMENT

- Minimum two players
- Joker cards / red cones

DIRECTIONS

1. Each player has two joker cards.
2. Players play points.
3. At the end of each point, a player can use a joker card.
4. If they lose the point, they could steal the point from their opponent.
5. If they have won the point, they win two points.
6. Players can only use two cards per set.
7. Play to 10 points.

THE LAST POINT WINS

EQUIPMENT

- Minimum two players
- stopwatch

DIRECTIONS

1. Players play points.
2. The coach sets a random time limit on the stopwatch.
3. The players can't see the time.
4. When the stopwatch runs out, whoever wins the last point wins the match.

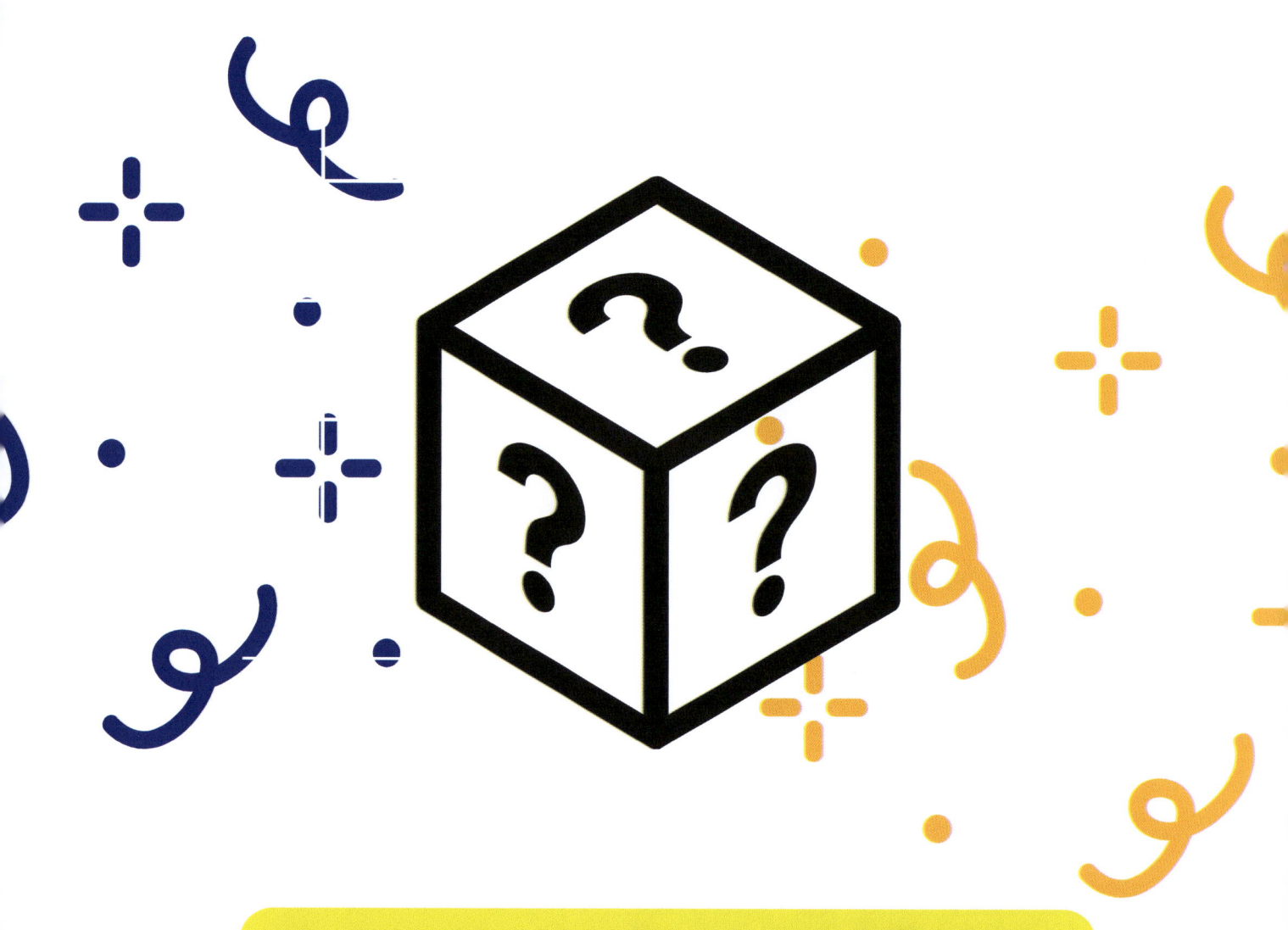

RANDOM NUMBER!

EQUIPMENT

- Minimum two players
- Ten sided die

DIRECTIONS

1. Players roll the die, and whatever number they get, that's how many points they need to win the set.
2. Player A may roll 10.
3. Player B may roll 2.
4. Player A needs 10 points to win, and player B needs 2.
5. After the set, the player rolls again.

I'M IN!

EQUIPMENT

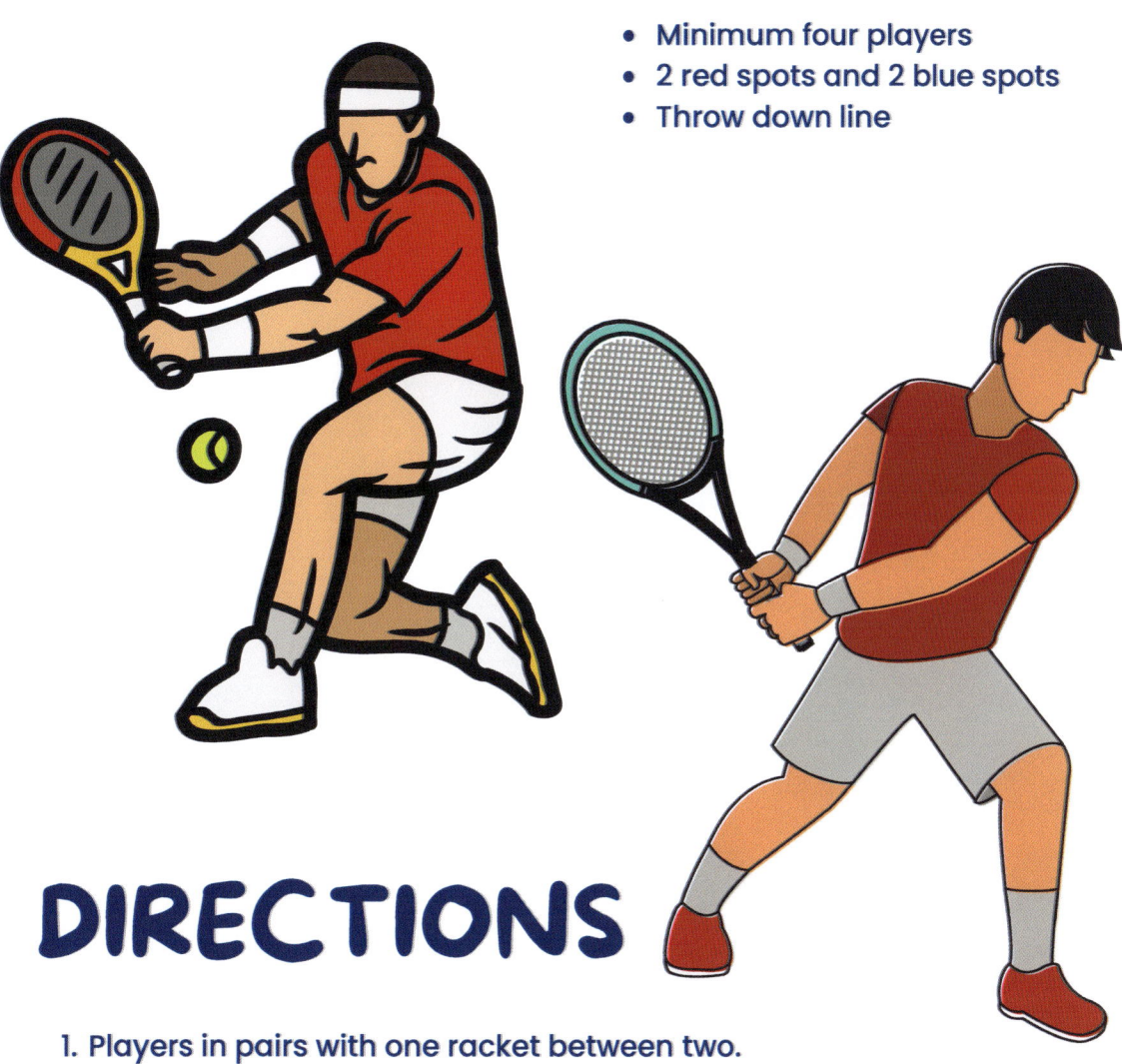

- Minimum four players
- 2 red spots and 2 blue spots
- Throw down line

DIRECTIONS

1. Players in pairs with one racket between two.
2. Players number themselves one and two.
3. Player one starts on the court.
4. Player two stands behind the baseline in a safe position.
5. Player one starts the point.
6. The opposite team do the same.
7. Either player two can shout 'I'm in', and they take control of the point from player one.

FRENEMIES

EQUIPMENT

- Minimum two players

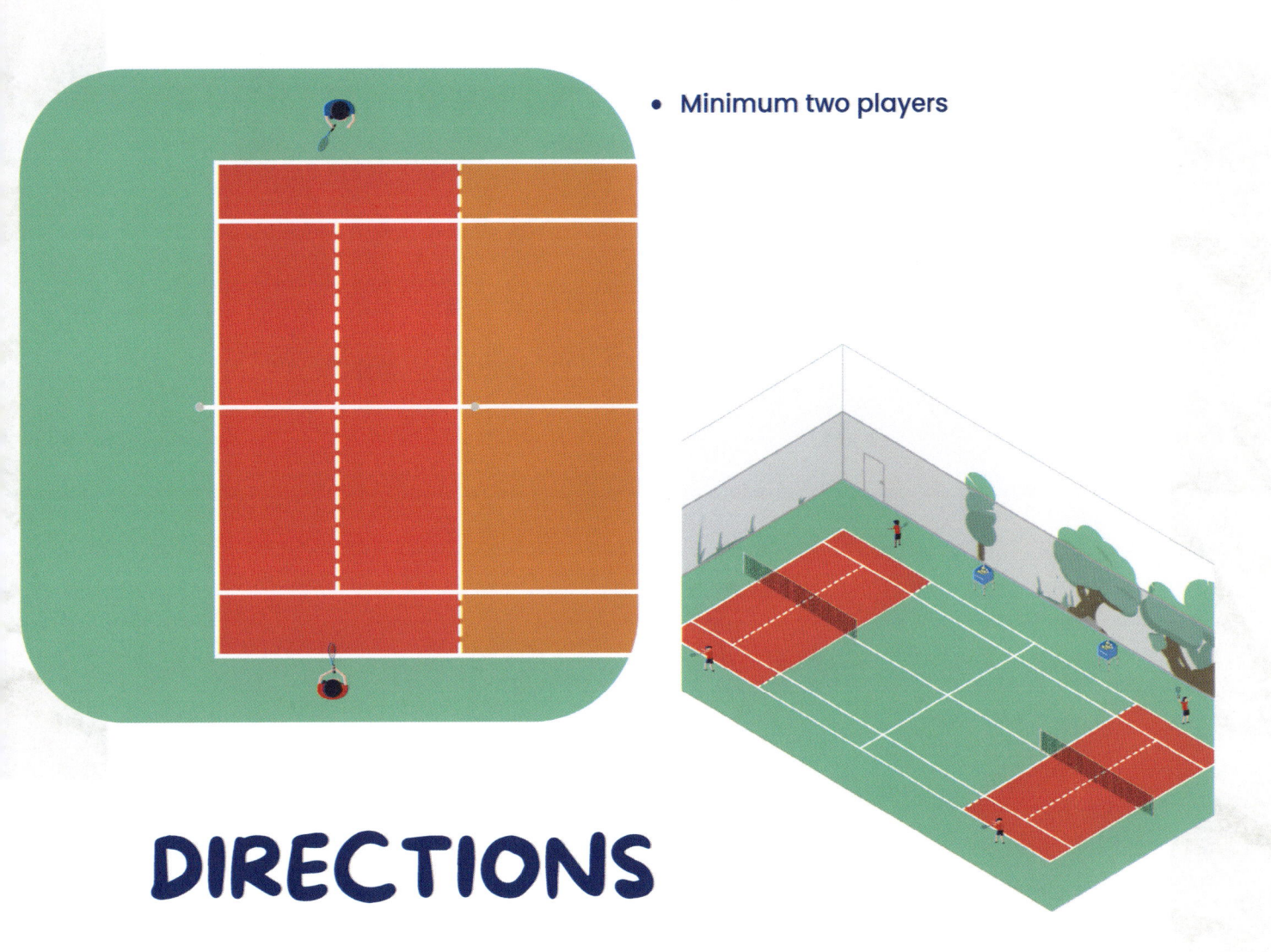

DIRECTIONS

1. Players work in pairs.
2. One player starts the rally with a serve.
3. Players must work cooperatively as friends to get a set target, i.e. 2.
4. Once they reach 2, they become enemies and play the point out.
5. Next, the other player will start, and the friendship rally increases to 3 (or you can improve by any number the kids want).

BOUNTY HUNTER

EQUIPMENT

- Minimum two players
- Twenty cones

DIRECTIONS

1. Each player begins with ten cones.
2. Before each point, a player places a 'bounty' on the outcome of the point.
3. The other player must match or raise the bounty to play the point.
4. The players play the point; whoever placed the bounty serves.
5. The winner gets all the bounty.
6. The other player now has the opportunity to set the bounty.
7. You can either play one round and rotate the players, or they can play the best of three sets.
8. The game is based on players feeling momentum and confidence.

ROCK, PAPER, SCISSORS

EQUIPMENT

- Minimum four players

DIRECTIONS

1. Players in pairs and each pair are a division.
2. Players play timed points but don't keep score.
3. At the end of the time, they must compete on a rock, paper or scissors match.
4. The winner moves up to the next division.
5. The loser moves down.
6. This is a fun way of introducing winning and losing to younger players.

MOOOOO OFF!

EQUIPMENT

- Minimum 4 players

DIRECTIONS

1. Players in pairs and each pair are a division.
2. Players play timed points but don't keep score.
3. At the end of the time, they must compete in a moo off!
4. The players both moo (like a cow) and the player who takes a breath or stops first loses.
5. The winner moves up to the next division.
6. The loser moves down.
7. This is another fun way of introducing winning and losing to younger players.

PEEL OFF

EQUIPMENT

- Minimum three players

DIRECTIONS

1. Players in 3's.
2. The player on their own is the controller.
3. This player sets a minimum rally number (1-4).
4. The three players rally until they reach that number.
5. Once they pass that freehold, the single player shouts 'life' and hits the ball to one of the opposite pair.
6. Those two players play the point out.
7. The other player 'peels' off and waits it out.

RESET!

EQUIPMENT

- Minimum 2 players

DIRECTIONS

1. Players play a tie break (7 or 10).
2. Each player has a reset button.
3. At any time during the match, they can call reset and go back to a previous score, i.e. I could call reset at 4-6 and choose to go back to 4-2.
4. After the first reset, the second player can only go back from the new score, i.e. 4-2 or earlier.
5. Allowing players to rewind the flow of a match.

LEVEL UP YOUR COACHING

@mytenniscoaching

MY TENNIS COACHING

YOUR COACH

STEVE WHELAN

Performance Coach and Coach Educator

Hi, I am your Tennis Coach. My name is Steve. I have been a full-time tennis coach for over twenty years and have been fortunate to work with beginners to national-level junior players.

Check out my website at **www.mytenniscoaching.com** to build your confidence, increase your knowledge and develop your coaching skills.

FREE WEBINARS

Try out my six free webinars today:

- How To Effectively Coach Technique
- Why Tactics Come Before Technique
- Constraint-Led Coaching
- The Best Drills for Beginners
- How to Coach Doubles
- 6 Common Coaching Challenges

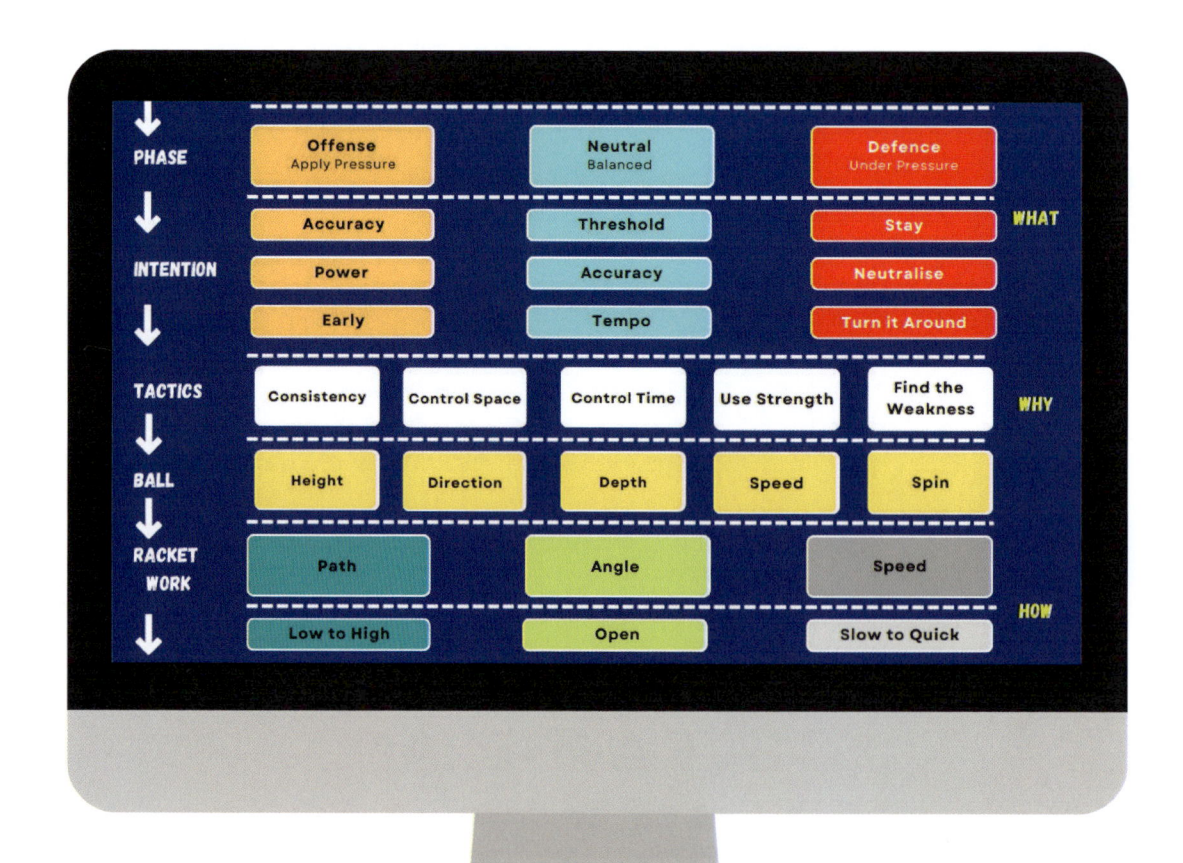

BECOME A BETTER COACH
WWW.MYTENNISCOACHING.COM

WANT TO BE A PERFORMANCE COACH!

3 THINGS YOU NEED

Confidence

CONFIDENCE means feeling sure of yourself and your abilities — not in an arrogant way, but in a realistic, secure way. Confidence isn't about feeling superior to others. It's a quiet inner knowledge of what you're capable of. Confident people: feel secure rather than insecure.

Knowledge

KNOWLEDGE applies to facts or ideas acquired by study, investigation, observation, or experience.

Skills

The ability to use one's knowledge effectively and readily in execution or performance. Tennis Coaches need to be able to communicate, demonstrate and organise effectively, and these are the core coaching **SKILLS** required to improve performance.

Ready for the challenge ?

BECOME A BETTER COACH

WWW.MYTENNISCOACHING.COM

MY MENTORING

READY TO TAKE YOUR COACHING TO THE NEXT LEVEL?

Need Confidence, knowledge or skills to get to the next level?

How about 24 hours of bespoke coach education content?
14 ebooks?
3 Hours private mentoring?
All online from your home?

BECOME A BETTER COACH
WWW.MYTENNISCOACHING.COM

MY TENNIS COACHING

COACH TESTIMONIALS

★★★★★

ALISON

Thanks for an enjoyable course, it's always very difficult to interact on zoom, however, I think you did a very good job and were very engaging.

★★★★★

DAN

Thanks for the course this morning. Very much enjoyed your way of presenting, lots of energy and engagement which kept things stimulating which I know is a real challenge in delivering courses online.

★★★★★

IVAN

Steve's communication skills are excellent. He not only passed on some great knowledge but made me fully understand the why

★★★★★

RICHARD

Steve, your presentation today was outstanding. This is the first time in 20 years I have given this level of feedback!

I truly hope you enjoy these games as much as your players will.

This book has been independently written, designed and edited by myself.

If you spot any errors or mistakes, please let me know below. I will make the necessary adjustments and send you an updated version for free.

CONTACT ME

🌐 www.mytenniscoaching.com

📷 @mytenniscoaching

✉ steve@mytenniscoaching.com

Printed in Great Britain
by Amazon